May the Wind Be at Your Back

ANDREW M. GREELEY

With Photographs by the Author

THE
SEABURY
PRESS

NEW YORK
A CROSSROAD BOOK

May the Wind Be at Your Back

The Prayer of St. Patrick

The Seabury Press
815 Second Avenue
New York, N.Y. 10017

Copyright © 1975 by The Seabury Press, Inc.
Cover and interior design by Carl Weiss
Printed in the United States of America

Library of Congress Catalog Card Number: 75-13523
ISBN: 0-8164-2595-7

For Lou and Collette Briody—may the wind, preferably from the south, always be at their backs.

FIRST MEDITATION

I arise to-day
Through a mighty strength, the invocation of
    Trinity,
Through a belief in the threeness,
Through confession of the oneness
Of the Creator of Creation. *

I roll out of bed in the morning protesting vigorously against the FM music and the grim weather forecast which alternate on my clock radio. I make the sign of the cross as the announcer begins the newscast. God knows one needs the sign of the cross because the news is always bad. My sinuses are blocked, my limbs are weary, my head is foggy, I'm not even sure what day it is; but I

---

*"Saint Patrick is supposed to have composed this hymn [of eight verses] and sung it to deceive assassins, lying in wait for him, into thinking that he and his companions were a herd of deer passing." (An Anthology of Irish Literature, edited by David H. Greene. New York: New York University Press. Volume I, 1971, p. 6.)

know there's a lot of work to be done. I'm probably already late.

The anger and confusion of my dream world is still stirring within me. I cannot remember what happened in my dreams, but I know I've done battle with foes, adversaries and enemies and other churlish creatures. Doubtless these creatures will reappear in the course of a day.

I want my tea.

Another day begins. It is a day of routine and monotony, of hasseling and harassing, of responsibilities and obligations, of time-consuming absurdities. I could get my work done if it only weren't for the telephone, the committee meeting, the pesty student, the bungling research assistant, that clown from Detroit who has called long distance to discuss something I said wrong in my column last Sunday. Go away, all you hasslers and harassers! I've got work to do.

And I still want my tea.

This isn't what life was supposed to be like. I didn't become a priest to fend off quacks and cranks, psychopathic ecclesiastics, and narcissistic academics. I love the Ford Foundation, but I do not want to have to fly to New York the day after tomorrow. It is a gray, dull day (I know this without even having to look). I spent a gray, dull night, and I am in a gray, dull mood. Could not the Lord God have produced a better world?

So I invoke the blessed Trinity—partly out of self-defense, partly out of habit, partly because there doesn't seem much else to do. Today will be like most days—lots of activity, little accomplished. I will not have much to show for my work at the end of it except an even more heavy weariness than when I began. Still I invoke the blessed Trinity with the sign of the cross. It is their world

as well as mine, and if it isn't much, it is the only one I've got. For all I know, it may be the only one they've got too. So we might just as well do the best we can with what we have. But if the Holy Spirit is brooding out there somewhere over Lake Michigan with "Ah! bright wings," I must confess I don't see any of the light.

And what day is this? What month? Where am I anyhow?

So having made my sign of the cross at the beginning of the day, I forget about the Blessed Trinity. Like many Christians and most Catholics of my generation, the doctrine of the Trinity is a millstone. We believe it, more or less, because it is part of our religion. It was something we learned that we had to believe under pain of mortal sin. "Father, Son, and Holy Spirit," that's it. If we are Christians we have to believe; we're Christians, so we believe it. It may have some abstract interest for us as a puzzle, but it doesn't seem very pertinent to anything in our daily lives. People once rioted in the streets over the doctrine of the Trinity. Queens and empresses and royal courtesans intrigued over the choice of words to express it. Bishops went into exile, armed bands of monks descended onto marketplaces in the desert to riot over it. Kingdoms were made and unmade, backstrairs politicians connived like precinct captains over the relationship of the Father and the Son. Christendom was split in two about whether the Holy Spirit proceeded from both the Father and the Son.

My God, they all must have been crazy!

Rioting, conniving, rebelling, intriguing over theological doctrine? How irrelevant can you get?

Patrick, at least, had the good taste just to mention the Trinity at the beginning and the end of "The Deer's Cry." (Unlike his contemporary, Athanasius, who spread the paradox of the Trinity

[10]

out over the interminable verses of the *Athanasian Creed,* which we used to mindlessly rush through in the Breviary.) The issue today is not oneness, or threeness, or anythingness but is there a God at all? Does life have any purpose at all? Is the early morning ''blahs'' really what the cosmos is all about? Ennui—is that the nature of the universe, and is hell really nothing more than other people? Even those who purport to be Christians aren't so sure any more. They repeat the proper phrases and recite the proper creed, but they find themselves either rejecting the possibility of understanding and turn to raw emotion for religious kicks or bog down in agnosticism as they try to wrestle with the most primary and elemental questions long before they get to the issue of the one or the three. Athanasius lived in a relatively stable universe; he could afford to worry about the paradoxes of the Trinity. Patrick (or the writer who put ''The Deer's Cry'' in Patrick's mouth) may have been a relatively unlettered missionary on the damp, Gaelic fringes of civilization; but he could be confident about the nature of the universe, about the accessibility of God, about the purpose of human life. For him, the mystery about the one and the three was not something to be repeated under pain of mortal sin; neither was it something to be repeated under pain of mortal sin nor a stumbling block, nor a philosophical puzzle. It was a resource, a strength, a powerful invocation with which to begin another day of determined and committed effort.

Hurray for Patrick and Athanasius and all the rest of them.

Unfortunately we are not they. We live in the twentieth century, in the moribund Enlightenment, the time when evolutionary optimism, secular progressivism, and liberal rationalism have all failed. It is the time when famine, eco-disaster, and apocalypse seem to impinge. Patrick and his followers had to worry only about the Danes; Athanasius and his staff had to be concerned only about the wild monks in the desert. We have to worry about ozone (too much in the cities and not enough in the stratosphere). What good is the Blessed Trinity to us? Either they made this mess and ought to be ashamed of themselves, or they didn't make it and don't exist, and there's not much we can do about things.

Come to think of it, maybe my best bet would be to go back to bed for another hour.

Those of us who are more hopeful assume that somewhere theologians have "updated" the doctrine of the Trinity. Certainly theologian Karl Rahner has rearticulated in one of his obscure volumes the doctrine of the Trinity, or I bet halfway through the book *Insight* (which I've got to try to read again someday) Bernard Lonergan has addressed himself to the subject. So even if I don't know what in the world the doctrine of the Trinity means or how it could possibly be pertinent to my life, at least some people somewhere know that it is not as absurd as it sounds.

What was it about the doctrine of the Trinity that was worth fighting and dying for so long ago? Aquinas and Augustine and the great theologians merely articulated something which at that stage of the game seemed to have been very vital and dynamic for the ordinary faithful. The Blessed Trinity apparently got tied up in the straitjacket of rigid academic theology where repeating the right phrases was far more important than understanding the message. The God of whom Jesus spoke does not seem to be the sort of personage (or personages) who could reveal something to "try our faith" or to "teach us humility" or to impose on us a new obligation "under pain of mortal sin." So there must be some point behind the mystery of the Trinity, one which our predecessors understood and we don't. The doctrine of the Trinity may well convey some glorious, spectacular religious truth that they grasped and we missed.

It is possible, of course, that they were howling savages, irrational barbarians, superstitious freaks. Modern history began the year we were born, didn't it? Could anything important have happened before us? Could any good have come out of fourth-century Alexandria or fifth-century Ireland? Would you want Patrick or Athanasius in your encounter session?

Mysteries are supposed to be revelations, illuminations, secrets, break-throughs into the hidden wisdom of the universe. Those who believe in the doctrine of the Trinity thought they had discovered a secret of unparalleled richness and importance. They felt about it the way we would feel if suddenly we found out the secret of nuclear fusion energy to eliminate pollution and shortage for all human time. For them the revelation of the Trinity was a break-through into the hard inner core of meaning behind the universe. Patrick invoked the Trinity when he rose from bed in the morning not because he was afraid he would commit mortal sin if he did not, but because the secret of the Trinity was a brilliant, dazzling illumination which routed the cold, gloomy clouds of Ireland, as well as the even more cold and gloomy clouds of pagan superstition and ignorance. Patrick truly rose in the power of the Trinity and worked the day long reinforced by that power.

Did he know something we don't?

He was nothing particularly special—a runaway slave, not too well educated, with personal faults and frailties that he was quite willing to acknowledge. He was definitely a lesser monk in his own community. Everybody knew that he had this crazy dream about going back to Ireland and converting the pagans and savages there to Christianity (a thankless task at best), but no one in the monastery took Patrick and his dream very seriously. Nor did they expect that ecclesiastical authority would ever authorize such a crazy mission.

And they may not have. It is altogether possible that Patrick went to Ireland pretty much on his own, or with only the slightest hint of ecclesiastical approval (although they certainly gave it in retrospect). Even by his own self-description, Patrick was not the kind of man one would choose to lead a maximum effort to convert a new nation—particularly one as difficult as Ireland was even in those days.

So when this quite ordinary, even mediocre, man took it upon himself to do battle with the contentious and cantankerous pagan Irish he needed all the help he could get. Somehow, some way that we find difficult to understand, the invocation of the Trinity at the beginning of the day energized what even through the mists of legend and uncertainty turned out to be one of the most extraordinarily successful missionary ventures in all of human history. (For almost two thousand years it has been virtually impossible even for their own clergy and hierarchy to drive the Irish out of the Church—though more recently in the United States efforts in this direction have achieved limited success.)

What, then, did Patrick see in the Trinity? Can we in our own terms find illumination that corresponds to our anxiety and anguish, and ambiguity in the revelation that in God there is threeness and oneness. If the doctrine of the Trinity is not a contradiction to test our faith or a paradox to baffle us but an illumination to help us, it may just be possible that there is enough common humanity between us and our predecessors for us to find illumination in the doctrine of the Trinity just as they did.

The insight which our ancestors put into words in the Trinitarian councils at the beginning of the history of the Church can be expressed in contemporary terms by the assertion that God is relational. We find it very difficult to cope with the philosophical term and the philosophical mentality expressed in the word "consubstantial"; but we all know what "relational" means. For weal or woe, however, this profound and illuminating insight was first expressed in a philosophical system in which "consubstantial" meant something. If one were to use "relational" then to express the same insight to Patrick and his contemporaries, they would have been as baffled as we are by "consubstantial."

The doctrine of the Trinity reveals to us that the Deity is an intense network of relationships. God is not only personal, He is interpersonal; He is not only love, He is communal love, interacting love, love flowing over and becoming itself a reality. God is not stasis, He is action; He is not a static, immobile Being but a dynamic, moving, initiating, responding, interacting Being. There is even more activity going on within the relational network of the Deity than there is going on in the heart of the atom.

The God of the Christians is not the unmoved First Mover of Aristotle or the disembodied abstract Idea of Plato, though he shares some of the qualities of both. Because our later theology has used so much Greek philosophical terminology, we have forgotten the stark contrast between the Universal Idea and the Unmoved Mover on the one hand and the Blessed Trinity on the other. The

Mover and the Idea are abstract, aloof, uninvolved, disinterested. The Trinity is involved. It is relational externally (vis-à-vis us) because it is relational internally (vis-à-vis itself). The God of the Christians was a living God, a God of feeling, compassion, action, a God who not merely watched but also initiated and responded. The Scriptures make this clear. The Father sent the Son, the Son returned to the Father, the two of them would send the Holy Spirit. There was a lot of activity going on in the divine area. The Christians came out of the apostolic time absolutely convinced of the dynamism of the divinity. It took them several hundred more years to find a way to articulate the insight in philosophical terms that were precise enough not to be misunderstood by their contemporaries. We have been too content to rest on their laurels, perhaps. A major philosophical and theological task now faces us. We must find a way to rearticulate the insight that there is a lot of activity going on in God in terms that are as precise in our time as the Trinitarian terms were fifteen hundred years ago. We must do so not because it is an interesting philosophical challenge (though it is) or because we can at last make God perfectly understandable (we cannot any more than our predecessors could), but because the insight that our God is a dynamic, active, loving God is too important a one to be lost or buried under rigid and obsolescent technical categories.

There are profound philosophical issues at stake, and this booklet is not the place to raise them. It does seem to me, however, that the process philosophy of Alfred North Whitehead provides one framework in which this rearticulation of the Trinitarian insight can take place. Whitehead's notion of the distinction between God's "antecedent" nature and his "consequent" nature seems to me to touch on the same aspect of the Ultimate Reality that the early

Christians experienced in and through Jesus: God is active, dynamic, relational. Whitehead would go further and say that God is growing, moving, suffering, changing. To those of us steeped in Greek philosophical modes of thinking about God, such terms seem dangerous. Some Catholic theologians, however, are prepared to argue that the Whitehead categories are not contrary to traditional Christian teaching, and indeed they may well be a better way than Aristotelian categories to articulate the insights of the Scripture.

But these are complex, abstruse—though extremely important —philosophical questions. The critical point is that when I rise from my restless conflicted sleep in the morning and make the sign of the cross, I am doing more than just linking myself with the past, more than just reasserting a traditional doctrine, more than just mouthing a phrase which seems to have no meaning. I am asserting that the God I believe in is a dynamic, creative, active, living, loving God. And when I assert that I imply that the universe produced by Him is animated by that dynamic, active, living Love which is the core of His network of relationships. If God is relational, then so is the universe; if God is Love, then so is the cosmos. It is not random, absurd chance; it is not dull, drab, dreary, dreadful days; it is not absurdity, not a tale told by an idiot, full of sound and fury, signifying nothing. It is a relationship.

Life is romance. My life is a love affair, a response to an invitation to love that was proffered by the very fact that I came into existence. Patrick knew that when he woke up in the morning. He might have used different words to express what he knew, but the same insight is available to me when I wake up in the morning. When I make the sign of the cross I can permit myself to be dazzled by the astonishing illumination of a loving, relational God. If I become sufficiently dazzled, I can go forth into the world and dazzle others. I need not growl at the traffic as I crawl toward my office, I need not grump at the people who meet me at the door and glower as I walk down the corridor to my office, snarling at my colleagues who should chance to encounter me (though, to tell the truth, generally they are not there yet). I need not be hassled by the telephone or harassed by pests; I need not be put off by psycho-pathic bishops and narcissistic professors. I can laugh off the harass-ments and feel compassion for the pests. The sign of the cross in the morning is more than just a way of waking up, it is more than just a brief interlude before I get to the teapot or pour the milk onto the Granola. The invocation of the Trinity in the morning is a transformative experience, one that can make me over, illumine my day, and, if I listen to and believe its revelation, make me to be-come truly part of Patrick's deer herd in my daily life.

Maybe I'll begin tomorrow. Now I simply have to have my tea.

SECOND
MEDITATION

I arise to-day
Through the strength of Christ's birth with His
baptism,
Through the strength of His crucifixion with His
burial,
Through the strength of His resurrection with His
ascension,
Through the strength of His descent for the
judgement of Doom.

The wind howls in off the lake. You can with some effort see across the street. Station KW 039, the dutiful tool of the U. S. Weather Service, reports the cold-wave warnings, as though it were not cold enough already. The waters of Lake Michigan are rampaging, tearing up beaches and dunes as though destruction were more fun than gentle shaping and reversing. I am up, I have my tea; but there is every indication that this is a day when I should much better have stayed in bed. I do not want to leave my room. There may not be assassins laying in wait for me, as there were often enough for Patrick and his companions when they first sang the deer cry hymn. This day is obviously going to be so bad that one would venture into it at considerable risk. Cold, darkness, snow, wind are merely the physical symbols of a distinctly unpleasant place. My room is warm and cozy; the TV works, I have a stack of records to listen to, a stack of books to read, cheese and salami to eat, a bottle of Double-

Century sherry to sip. I'm sorry, world, I'm going to turn you off along with my telephone. There are too many risks and dangers, too many discomforts and annoyances, too many affronts and harassments out there. Go 'way, humankind. I'm staying here with my books, records, and cheese.

I have obligations and responsibilities. Sure. Doesn't everyone? But just for today, I want to betray them all. I want to become invisible, I want to escape from people; I want to be left alone.

Yes, that's what it's all about. I want to be left alone.

"Aha!" says the reader. "Typical priest. Married people with children can't even afford the luxury of thinking about being left alone."

Baloney, says I.

Show me someone who doesn't experience almost daily temptation to lock himself into his room and turn off the world and I'll show you a mysterious visitor from outer space who has donned human garb. For it is the nature of being human not to want to leave your room sometimes—whether it be stashed with sherry and cheese or not.

We don't like responsibilities, and it doesn't matter whether we are laity, religious or cleric. We all want to be left alone. Somehow or other we have acquired responsibilities, mostly without asking for them, frequently without even thinking about them; and having acquired them, alas, we cannot shed them. The responsibilities may vary from person to person, but we all have them. We would at times dearly like to be rid of them for one day a week, or one day a month, or even one day a year.

One eats one's breakfast, drinks a last cup of tea, reads the

morning newspapers, turns off the phone and crawls back into the blessed oblivion of bed. Oh bliss unalloyed, oh joy supreme, oh experience without parallel!

Like Patrick rounding up his crowd to continue their journey, assassins or no, I'm going out into the cold into my ugly orange Volkswagon to fight my way down the even more ugly Ellis Avenue to find my way to our beleaguered research center which is called, not for nothing, the Woodlawn Holiday Inn. I am going to do it in part (a very small part, I fear) because I am virtuously committed to what I am doing, in part (a larger part) out of sheer habit, and in part (unspecified) because I'd be afraid not to. The ice and the sludge, the snow and the cold, the affronts and the harassments have to be risked. Why? The only answer most of us can give is because they are there. We have to do what we have to do, and that's that. So off into the cold we go. One can no more remain in one's room sipping sherry, munching cheese, and listening to Gustav Mahler than one can live in Chicago and avoid cold, snowy winters. It is written that thou shalt go to work regardless.

But Patrick would have us believe that we go out into the world to work with *strength,* the strength of Christ's birth, baptism, crucifixion, burial, resurrection, and his ultimate return.

God knows I need strength, strength to stay awake, strength to control my temper, strength to avoid moods, strength to smile and laugh, strength not to feel like quitting when something fails, strength not to be disheartened by the harsh words, the envy, the dislike, the animosity that greets me when I go out into the world. You can't get through a day of life without spiritual strength. It's a truism, of course, that Christ brings us strength. I have been hearing that since first grade. But life is still terribly difficult, or so it seems when I first put on my scarf and gloves to leave the Double-Century and the brie and venture forth into the cold light of the winter day. I need more strength, it seems, to cope with the monotony, the ordinariness of life than I do to deal with its major challenges. Dangerous assassins are not the ones that lurk behind the rocks and bushes to threaten my life; my assassins are those that are built into the fabric of my existence—weariness, monotony, routine, frustration, discouragement.

Could Patrick write a deer cry which would enable me to sneak by those assassins without being attacked?

Doubtless the honored saint would respond by saying that the hymn he and his colleagues sang (perhaps whistled in the dark to keep their courage up) is adequate for dealing with any assassin—a wild Irishman with a rock or the enervating, preying cancer of ordinariness. I suspect even Patrick would admit that under normal circumstances you don't have to contend with rock-throwing assassins every day even in Chicago; but you do have to contend with ordinariness every day, no matter where you live.

In either case Patrick would surely insist one must turn to the Lord Jesus for strength. Fair enough, Patrick, but having turned to the Lord Jesus, what comes next?

Patrick knew substantially less about Jesus than we do. Indeed, we know more about him, we see him more clearly, we understand him more accurately, we comprehend him more fully than any generation since those who knew him personally. The immense body of biblical scriptural scholarship which has been built up through the years of the last centuries gives us a much greater knowledge of the person of Jesus and his message than was available to almost all our predecessors in the Christian faith. While at one time such scriptural scholarship seemed to be anti-Christian, now in fact it has become clear that the scholarship enables us to understand Jesus better than he was ever understood before. We are far closer to him, at least in our ability to hear him, than was Patrick or any other man of his era. We can hear Jesus more clearly, of course, without understanding him better.

Patrick and most of the other saints of the last fifteen hundred years would have failed the test in modern scriptural scholarship. They would have had only the most simple and elementary notions about the historical context in which Jesus lived and worked. They might completely misunderstand the point and purpose of many of the parables, and they might not at all be able to distinguish between the theological reflections of the Evangelists and the core of the historical traditions they are reporting. In every imaginable way, then, they would be considered inferior to us in their knowledge about Jesus. If only knowledge guaranteed virtue!

Patrick was not impeded notably by his low level of scriptural sophistication or by his ignorance of the history of religious or what must be considered his primitive exegetical skills. Somehow the real Jesus still managed to get through to him to him through the Scriptures, while the real Jesus frequently does not get through to us. We may have sorted out all the forms, the genres, the redactions, and the traditions to be found in the New Testament stories; we know *about* Jesus, Patrick knew him.

I do not write these things to criticize scriptural scholarship, which I think is one of the most important religious scholarly disciplines of our era. Patrick and his contemporaries would have been well served if they had had available to them the immense resources and richness of scriptural scholarship that are available to us. I simply say that they didn't need these things; we who have them need something more important, something that Patrick had in great measure.

Like faith.

For that is where one gets strength from Jesus—through faith. Patrick found strength in the coming of Jesus to Bethlehem, in his self-disclosure on the banks of the Jordan River, in the horrible agony of his death and burial, in the bright glory of his resurrection, and in the solemn promise of his return. Patrick believed that Jesus spoke truly and accurately and authentically of his heavenly Father. Jesus was not just an historical figure to be studied (though he is surely that); Jesus was a messenger from God. If one believed the message the messenger brought, ah, then one indeed had immense strength to struggle with the weariness and difficulty of human life. If one really believed the things that Jesus came to preach . . . well, it would still be hard to turn off the Mahler and be about one's responsibilities, but one could do it, and not reluctantly but gladly, graciously, hopefully, elegantly because one would know that one was about great things.

In a life transformed by the revelation of Jesus there is no such thing as ordinariness or monotony—at least not for very long.

From Bethlehem to the Parousia the life of Jesus stands as a message of promise and hope, of promise fulfilled, of promise being fulfilled, of promise still to be fulfilled.

The first promise comes in the gift of creation of life itself, both the superabundant life that flows in and through the universe and the fragile but terribly precious little life that is our own. When we experience life with even the slightest self-consciousness we realize that it is a promise of something better, a promise, as theologian

Gregory Baum has put it, that tomorrow will be different. The prophecies, the promises, the history of the Old Testament are a reflection and an articulation of this primordial promise that we experience as being coextensive with life itself. In Bethlehem when Jesus came, on the Jordan River when he revealed himself at the beginning of his public life, the first promise was fulfilled. Life was indeed about something better, something more, something grand, glorious, supreme, astonishing.

And in the death, burial, resurrection, and ascension of Jesus a new promise began to be fulfilled and is still being fulfilled today, a promise that humankind could break from sin and suffering, that it could live by love and hope, that it could put aside hatred, enmity, conflict, that it could enjoy and rejoice in its splendid plurality and diversity. Jesus said that he came that we might have life and have it more abundantly; it is the promise of this more abundant life that is presently being fulfilled slowly, gradually, haltingly, sometimes against insuperable odds. Still, the promise of more abundant life is being fulfilled.

Finally, there is a promise yet to be fulfilled, the most basic and fundamental promise of all, that somehow, someway, some day, good will triumph over evil, life over death, love over hatred, joy over sadness, comedy over tragedy completely, utterly, and totally. In the promise of the Second Coming of Jesus we articulate this conviction of ours that life does matter and that someday it will triumph over death absolutely.

So it is in the promises of Jesus that Patrick found and any Christian can find strength. The length and the depth, the height and the breadth of that promise can be better understood, perhaps, if we know more about the Scriptures; but one can read the New Testament in all its complexities and confusions with little if any scholarly knowledge and still learn of these promises. If one believes these promises, then one lives, lives in an extraordinary and fantastic way, lives like no one who does not accept the promises can know. One does not live perfectly, one does not live as a child of promise all the time; indeed, the struggle between the promise and despair is an endless one in each person's life. If one believes the promise at all, even some of the time, one becomes a different kind of human being at least for that brief time of belief. It is in the strength and promises of Jesus, the promise fulfilled, the promise being fulfilled, and the promise to be fulfilled, that Patrick found the strength that we who are his colleagues also find our strength. There was no way Patrick could avoid travelling the road where the assassins lurked; there is no way I can escape going off to work today. My romance with the brie, the Double-Century, and Mahler is fantasy. I shall go to work today and so shall the rest of you. We will not shirk our responsibilities, we will not, like some bizarre character in a Victorian novel (or a half dozen monsignors I know), take to our beds for the rest of our lives. We will do what we have to do.

The big question is why do we do what we have to do? The reason why we do it will tell us how we do it. Patrick went down the road with a song on his lips and joy in his heart because his journey was part of the promise being fulfilled. So, too, we go to work each day, we take on the responsibilities of our lives every morning not merely because we have to, not merely because we have no choice, not merely because we would be overwhelmed by guilt feelings if we didn't; we take on the obligations, the responsibilities of each day with a song on our lips and joy in our hearts because we realize that somehow and in some way our daily responsibilities are linked with the fulfillment of promise. We do what we have to do, but we do it graciously, generously, joyously, elegantly, because what we have to do is a response to the promise and a partial fulfillment of it. Our work does not become easy, the monotony does not dissipate, the routine does not end, the dreariness is not swept away; the snow and ice are still there, the wind still howls, the lake still pounds the shore; but in the birth and baptism, the death and burial, the resurrection and ascension, and the coming of Jesus once again, all of these things are transformed. The storms will end, the snow will melt, the clouds will drift away and the warmth of the love of God as revealed in the promises of Jesus will bring to birth a spring that will never end.

THIRD
MEDITATION

I arise to-day
Through the strength of the love of Cherubim,
In obedience of angels,
In the service of archangels,
In hope of resurrection to meet with reward,
In prayers of patriarchs,
In predictions of prophets,
In preachings of apostles,
In faiths of confessors,
In innocence of holy virgins,
In deeds of righteous men.

I arrive in my office. Into the wastebasket with the telephone messages my secretary has so diligently transcribed. If they want me badly enough they'll call back (except the Ford Foundation, which we dial immediately, of course). Into the wastebasket with half the mail. Ah, what do we have here? A letter from a seminarian. He is angry with me. Is it my opposition to liberation theology? No. Is it my skepticism about Pentecostalism? No. Is it my support for Richard J. Daley? No. It is none of these mortal sins that has angered the young man. He is angry because I have written a column saying that I could understand why ministers leave the ministry because of weariness.

Not so long ago, criticism of resigning priests would bring a deluge of letters from seminarians who viewed the departing broth-

ers as folk heroes. Now one speaks a gentle word of sympathy for those who have left the active ministry and another generation of seminarians becomes upset. If one lives long enough every pendulum swings back.

The young man is dismayed because I do not challenge the resigning cleric with his commitment, with the vision of the priesthood, with the excitement of the gospel, with the splendor of his vocation.

Like I say, you wait long enough. . . .

The seminarian is very young and very enthusiastic. He does not understand how I can be sympathetic with the weary priest because he has never been tired himself. It would be impossible for me to respond to him (though I shall write him in any event) with words that would have any meaning for him. Until you have been weary, you don't know what it is like; and after you've been weary yourself, you can sympathize with and understand almost anything that a person does who is in the grip of weariness. You don't approve necessarily, you don't plan to take the same path; but you can understand.

Weariness is physiological first of all. The body is not as strong and flexible as it used to be. It doesn't bound back the way it once did. It takes two days to get over an airplane trip; jet lag lasts ten days instead of five; you can cope with only one half-day of a professional meeting when a week was not too long years ago; any committee session that goes beyond a half hour becomes intolerable. One grows old.

But the worst part of weariness is not physiological at all. You can be in excellent physical condition, get a good night's sleep every night, eschew drinking, smoking, and the ingestion of other noxious substances and be in the prime of physical condition. One still grows weary.

It is not the tenth teenager who is caught stealing a car that gets to you, but the hundredth. It is not the fiftieth nutty young couple who thinks the whole adult world is wrong about their romance but the five hundredth. It is not the five hundredth crank phone call but the five thousandth. It is not the fifth disastrous decision by Church leadership but the fiftieth.

It all piles up, and the feather that finally breaks the camel's back seems as heavy as a mountainside.

Weariness is repeated failure at everything you try. It is disgust with all the commitments you have made that turned out to be foolish. It is frustration with endless wasted hours on trivial and frivolous projects. It is rejection by others of what you think is the best you have. Weariness may not be hell, but it surely is purgatory.

When you are weary you don't quit completely; you are still capable of beginning again. Each September, each Christmastime, each Easter—those various times in the year when it is expected of us to begin again—we try valiantly, with various degrees of success, to reevaluate our commitments and projects and revalue ourselves. But too often we just go through the motions; we don't really believe there's any point in the motions. Our hearts are not in them, but we still do it because you've got to do something. The spark, the vitality has gone out of life; one still clings to life because it is all one has, but there's no fun left. Maybe the quitters are the smart ones; they at least don't pretend; they don't play any games or go through the motions of activity that is meaningless.

The weary person is beat, pounded into the ground, staggering around like George Forman after Muhammed Ali had knocked him to the floor. In such a daze, one can do almost anything.

And my young seminarian correspondent expects me to challenge such a person. Wait until he's forty!

The worst part about weariness is that you're alone.

It is of the essence of weariness that one is alone. Being alone both creates weariness and results from it. The more weary one is the more alone one feels, and the more alone one feels the worse the weariness becomes. It is not a matter of one's state in life. Celibates may not be alone and married people may be. The weariness of being alone comes to everyone; it is part of the human condition. For the committed celibate it is the feeling of being excluded from one's colleagues, one's friends, one's people, of having to face the burdens and difficulties of life completely cut off. It is in the midst of such profound existential loneliness that many celibates conclude that their celibacy is the cause of their weariness. But marriage is no cure for weariness. One can share the same bed with another every night and still feel weary and alone. One goes through the motions of loving and being loved, but they are superficial; they do not touch the core of one's personality. The weary married person may conclude that the marriage is responsible for weariness. Perhaps a new love will shatter the armor plate that seals off one's heart. So just as the celibate thinks that marriage may solve his problems, so the married person may think that another marriage will solve his. Both are wrong, but their error is understandable. The aloneness which comes from weariness travels with one wherever one goes and with whomever one lives. Another human person can divert us temporarily from our weariness; he or she cannot defeat weariness.

Another human can respond to our love, but the other person cannot create in us the capacity to love; and it is just that capacity that weariness destroys because it tells us in effect that love is impossible, or that if it were possible it would be dangerous. Routing weariness depends precisely on our rekindling our own capacity to give ourselves in love no matter how likely frustration and pain is to follow from such a gift. Weariness goes away when love is rediscovered.

So Patrick tells us that we are not alone, that we have clustered around us such improbable creatures as the cherubim, angels, and archangels; that the patriarchs are praying for us, the prophets predicting for us, the apostles preaching for us, and the confessors, virgins, and the holy people are all on our side.

We are tempted to say, so what? How many precincts can Jacob deliver? What good is Osee in the face of the world food crisis? How can St. James the Less bring savor back into my life? Michael, Gabriel, Raphael and the other angels, should they exist at all, seem to be busy about many other things. Why should they have any time for me? The confessors, the holy virgins, and the righteous men may be splendid folk, but they have no more clout in the ecclesiastical power structure now than they did in their own lifetimes. The same psychopaths who hounded them are presently alive and well, and now they are as often inside the Church as outside of it.

There was a time when being associated with the prophets, the patriarchs, the apostles, the cherubim and the rest of that crowd seemed to mean something. People had a sense of the community between the Church Militant and the Church Triumphant. Well, the Church Triumphant has gone out of fashion and the Church Militant has yielded to the Church in Dialogue. The prophets and patriarchs, angels and apostles, holy women and righteous men were doubtless splendid and admirable creatures, but they are not around just now, and we do not have the sense of their near presence that our predecessors did—perhaps as short a time ago as fifty or sixty years. They are (one trusts they would excuse the word) irrelevant.

Our knowledge of history is like our knowledge of the Scriptures. We know far more about it than those who went before us did; but we get far less out of it.

Our ancestors knew rather little history. They painted biblical personages—patriarchs, prophets, and apostles—as though they were men and women who lived in the same culture and the same historical epoch in which they lived. Abraham became a minor German princeling, Peter a cardinal in lay garb, Mary an Italian mother. The artists would have admitted the inaccuracy of the ethnic link, but they would not have understood any suggestion that the culture of Renaissance Italy was very different from that of First Temple Jerusalem. Men like Patrick had very little sense of who their predecessors were, how they lived, and what they were interested in. The very strong possibility that the prophet Amos was not the dirt farmer he seemed to be but rather a petty landed aristocrat would have been deemed quite trivial and frivolous information by Patrick. For us it is very important; we cannot deal with our predecessors unless we can fill out survey questionnaires about who they were and what they were up to.

But our knowledge of history seems to isolate us from those who went before us instead of uniting us. Patrick and his contemporaries knew very little history and very little about the prophets and the patriarchs and the apostles and the righteous men, but they felt they knew them and could easily rally together with them in the common cause. Patrick and his deer pack could go down the road seemingly defenseless but quite confident that there were invisible armies operating all around them. When we go down the road we go down it alone.

Even though he knew little history, Patrick was well aware that he was the product of a history. Who he was and where he stood was the result of the efforts of the prophets, the patriarchs, the apostles, the confessors, the righteous men and the holy virgins. Abraham, Jude, Thaddeus, Timothy, Thekla, Cecilia—they all had cleared the way for him; they passed on down to him what he was preaching to the rambunctious barbarians of Erin. They were his spiritual ancestors, he was their spiritual child. The problems he faced were those they faced; the resources that aided them were available to him. Patrick was not superstitious, in all likelihood. He didn't really imagine that the archangel Michael and a band of cherubs were lurking down by the crossroads at the river (though he would not have excluded the possibility). The strength Patrick drew from his predecessors was not so much from a conviction of their physical presence as from an understanding of continuities. He was part of the same tradition they were; he was where their faith had enabled him to be; he believed in the same Lord, followed the same Jesus, faced the same dangers, relied on the same strengths and supports of the gospel he preached. What more does it take, Patrick might have asked, to have a sense of community with someone else?

But we have a very hard time thinking that way. We are conscious not of continuities but of discontinuities, not of communion but of separation, not of similarities but of differences. Even if we are not part of the "New Politics" generation, who seem to believe that real history began the year they were born, we still have a hard time taking our predecessors very seriously. The dogma of evolutionary progress so pervades our cultural environment that we almost take it for granted that anyone who lived before 1930 was a superstitious savage. Ours is the first generation to be guilty of temporal ethnocentrism, the assumption that we are so superior intellectually, morally, and spiritually to our predecessors that we have little if anything to learn from them and almost nothing in common with them. Job, Bartholomew, Ezekiel, Raphael, Gregory and Lucy, even Patrick, Brigid, Columcille, and that crowd were splendid people, but they didn't know about Freud or Marx or Darwin. They had no opportunity to watch John Chancellor or Walter Cronkite, they didn't know about the second law of thermodynamics, they had never seen a jet airplane or a moon rocket launch or pictures of the mushroom cloud after the bomb dropped. What could we possibly learn from them?

On the contrary, the tradition, if it is anything at all for us, is a burden, an obstacle rather than an asset. We are embarrassed by the primitive naivete of our predecessors in the Church. We try to explain them if not explain them away; we try to systematically shed their world view and their perspective, and to address the human problems of contemporary life as though we were beginning completely afresh.

Thus it may be psychologically and culturally impossible for us to be as excited as Patrick was by the various bands of warriors who rallied around him and his deer pack as they went down the road bravely singing their hymn. We find that we must do our best to pretend that those bands of warriors have been safely committed by the Almighty to whatever regions of the hereafter reserved for those naive characters who lived before the secular saints, Darwin, Marx, and Freud.

Small wonder that we are alone.

At some other time in human history people will laugh at and ridicule us for our narrowness and rigidity and our inability to see two critical things:

1. We stand on the shoulders of our ancestors.
2. There are some fundamental human problems which do not change from generation to generation.

Thekla, Jude, Thaddeus, Zephaniah, Isaac—their ideas, their insights, their devotion, their courage helped to create the world of which we are a part. Our vision, our moral sensitivities, our dynamic energies are inheritances from the cultural past whether we like it or not. Freud, Marx, and Darwin could only have appeared in a culture formed in part by Abraham, Nathaniel, John the Divine, Augustine, Aquinas. Jet engines they didn't have, but a conviction that there was such a thing as history and that humankind could be part of its development, that the universe was rational and understandable, and that we were not merely defenseless slaves of nature —these are critical convictions without which our present civilization could not stand. Our predecessors may not have been as technically ingenious as we are, but they were philosophically far more brilliant and religiously far more sensitive.

But there is no reason to think that fear and loneliness, weariness and anxiety, discouragement and frustration, failure and disillusionment are any different now than they have ever been since homo sapiens began to be sapient. We may be able to explain electricity

[44]

while Patrick had no notion of it at all, but he may have been profoundly affected by a brilliant flash of lightning across the sky while we are serenely indifferent. Who is superior to whom?

If we can explain electricity, we cannot explain why there is anything at all, or what purpose those things that constitute our cosmos have if any. The proximate questions of meaning are more easily answered by our generation, but the ultimate issues are as obscure as they ever were. Patrick's faith and courage came from the conviction that there was purpose in the universe, that human history was not an aimless and irrational process, that God was at work in the world, and that all things and all events were somehow or other contributing to the completion of his purpose. Hence Patrick could march down the road with his deer pack serenely confident that *whatever happened* God's purpose would be served, and his life and mission would take its place in the lives and missions stretching from Abraham to St. Jerome.

With our superior "modern" mentality, we are apt to dismiss such a notion of God at work in human events as absurdly superstitious. We arrogantly assume that we were the first ones to come to that conclusion. In fact, the notion that God works through human history has seemed absurd to many who did not believe in every generation. It sounded as nutty to Patrick's pagan Irish audiences as it does to modern pagans. The contemporary Christian may need somewhat more sophisticated philosophical explanations of divine providence than did Patrick's deer pack. In fact, however, the leap of faith required to believe that God's plan is really working out down through the centuries of human existence is no greater for us than it was for Patrick.

It is purposelessness that causes weariness. If we have purpose, if our efforts do matter, if we are striving toward a goal that can be achieved and ultimately will be achieved, then we are no longer alone. We can truly begin again. Then we can open ourselves to the risks of loving and being loved. The political movements of our time—particularly Marxism—know this well. They promise their followers that there is purpose, that they can and will win, that history is on their side, and that it is therefore safe to take risks. The Marxist belief that one is part of an historical process is somehow more Christian than the temporal ethnocentrism of those Christians who see themselves having nothing in common with their ancestors. The Marxist, paradoxically enough, believes in continuity; the Christian frequently does not.

So we march down the deer path of our life, alone if we choose to be, weary if we want to be, discouraged if we are afraid to be anything else, isolated and cut off if we have no continuities with anyone who lives or anyone who has ever lived, and unable to love or be loved because the costs are too great and the outcome too uncertain.

That's a hell of a way to live.

Even if Patrick was wrong—and if we are Christians we "believe" he was right even if we don't "feel" it—it is much better to go down the path singing a hymn with companions both visible and invisible than it is to go down the path alone, muttering to ourselves because there is no one else to talk to.

FOURTH
MEDITATION

I arise to-day
Through the strength of heaven:
Light of sun,
Radiance of moon,
Splendor of fire,
Speed of lightning,
Swiftness of wind,
Depth of sea,
Stability of earth,
Firmness of rock.

I pick up my computer output.

We are studying mystical experience. I am endlessly fascinated by how widespread such experiences seem to be in the modern world (and how eager some of my colleagues in the social sciences are to deny that such experiences can be so common). If interludes of ecstatic joy still happen relatively often, then of course, the whole business about humankind kind evolving from the sacred to the secular must be jettisoned. The churches may be declining (serves 'em right, says I), but religion is not.

Still, I have never had such an experience, so while they fascinate me they also baffle me. I see the surface of things, that corrugated bark of the oak tree outside my window, the contrast of the white snow and the green of the natural Christmas tree, the lean and scrawny arms of the bush as it reaches up toward the slate gray

[49]

sky, the flash of red of the cardinal (bird, not ecclesiastic), the slush on the road—messy, sloppy, squishy, the black scar of the telephone line cutting across my early December picture postcard—those are all things one can see and feel. One can watch the evergreen tree shake in the strong northeast wind. That's real. One can hear the purr of the electric heater. That's real. One can feel the thud of the heavy lake waters against the dune. That's real.

But the mystics would say that those things aren't real at all, or that if they are, they are only real in a kind of minor real. Their reality comes from the power to reveal something that is "really real." As a sociologist, I'm prepared to agree with them that they have had an experience that for them brings them into contact with the "really real." As a Christian, I'm prepared to believe that there is a "Really Real" lurking out there somewhere. But the curve of the wave as it hits the sandbar, shattering itself into a million flakes of foam is nothing more for me, I fear, than water and force and energy doing their thing. For some, a wave may be a sacrament, but for me, a wave is a wave and nothing much else except an enjoyable sight perhaps.

Which is why I write prose instead of poetry.

This was not the case with Patrick, I think. He (or whoever wrote "The Deer's Cry") saw more in the sun, moon, the fire, lightning, wind, sea, earth, and the rock than I see. For these ordinary, natural things became for him sacraments, revelations. They had a reality of their own, indeed, but they spoke to him of a greater Reality, a deeper Reality, a richer Reality. The sun sits up there in the heavens (well, it's not up there today and hasn't been for a couple of weeks). It is a marvelous, fiery ball which moves across the sky every day. Sometimes it is quite high in the sky, and that means the weather will be warm and I can water ski tomorrow if the winds are calm. At other times it just barely peeks its head over the horizon, and that means the weather will be cold and any skiing will be done on snow.

I can find a book to tell me the heat of the sun, its chemical composition, when it was created, how it compares with the other stars in the universe (not too favorably, it turns out), and when the Second Law of Thermodynamics will seal its doom. That's the sun of the scientist.

But it's not my sun. Mine is the sun of the prose writer. I admire its power, I hunger for its light, I yearn for its warmth. I sorrow every time its setting moves a degree further south in the sky. But the sun is the sun is the sun. I need it, I like it, I want it; but unlike Patrick the light of the sun does not give me any spiritual strength. The sun is more than a glob of hot gas, but it is substantially less than a living witness.

Patrick, most of the saints, and all of the mystics see something more.

The moon is pretty as it hangs over my city at night (only relatively obscured by the sulfur dioxide). It's a nice decoration in the sky, but it does not speak to me of romance, much less of radiance. You have to have a certain way of looking at reality before the moon radiates. For me, it just kind of glows up there like a light bulb that's about to burn out. I do not deny the superior vision of those who see it as radiant, but it doesn't radiate for me.

Fire is warm, dazzling, dangerous. Fire may be something more than rapid oxidation, but for me it is something less than sacrament. I am awed by the lightning as it dances across the sky; it is more than just an electrical discharge, and I am willing to concede that it is an impressive show, but it is not a show of which I am conscious of being a part.

And so with the sea, the earth, the rock. I appreciate them all; I applaud their abilities; I acknowledge their importance. I freely concede that they are more than just chemical and mechanical processes, but for me they are not sacraments. I find in them impressive physical strength and I derive a sense of majesty from their power and force, but I do not find the spiritual and religious strength of which Patrick speaks in them. A rock is a rock, a tree a tree, a wave a wave; for me they are not sacraments.

There was a time when humans were alleged to have believed that everything was animate, that the sun, the moon, the sea, each rock and tree embodied a spirit. I am not so sure that I am completely persuaded that that's the way our "primitive" ancestors really thought. When they addressed a rock as though it had a spirit, as though it were capable of hearing what they said, I suspect that they may have been doing it with the full realization that the rock didn't hear the way humans heard. The animists were quite capable of making protoscientific use of water and air, fire and water. In their practical lives, they could distinguish clearly between objects as tools and objects as animated spirits. Their world view was different from ours, but perhaps not so different as their style of expression might suggest. I suspect that if we came along and told them that a rock had no spirit, they would look at us as though we were crazy. If we told them that we thought they lived in awe of the spirit of the rock and even worshipped it to some extent, they would look at us as though we were crazier still. If any dialogue in mutually meaningful categories could be carried on with our animist ancestors, we would probably discover that they thought the rock was a mysterious, marvelous thing which ought to be treated with reverence and respect. They would be greatly baffled if we told them it was not necessary to respect a rock or to look on it as a mystery, because after all it was nothing more than a collection of atomic force fields. From their primitive world view an atomic force field would be even more of a mystery than the rock.

But however one explains the "mythological" world view of our animist predecessors, they surely were much more readily disposed to see the animated rock as a revelation than are we, who think that once you have called something "a collection of atomic force fields" you have explained it in such a way that no mystery remains. Little children may still be fascinated by rocks, and they can be mystics; we adults know what a rock is—we can even analyze the geological layers in it—so there is no mystery left, no revelation possible. The rock is a rock is a rock even if the rock is Peter.

Is there some middle ground between the animist who sees the rock inhabited by a little spirit and the hyperscientist who sees the rock as an interacting system of electrons, neutrons, protons, and other dazzling, small particles? The prose writer like me can be impressed by the way it is unmoved as the waves of the lake shatter themselves against it, but the poet, the mystic, and a saint like Patrick see something more. The rock is for them a symbol, a mystery, a revelation, a sacrament. It tells them something about the granite-like strength of Being and of their own participation in that shatterproof granite.

The process goes something like this. We find ourselves in an interlude of existential need. The old way we looked at life no longer seems adequate. Our structured perceptions are unable to cope with the phenomena which impinge on our consciousness. We are worried, anxious, disturbed. Then we see a "thing," an object we have seen a thousand times before; but suddenly we see it for the first time. It takes possession of our consciousness momentarily; it shatters the old structures of our perception; it leaves our awareness, our consciousness temporarily open, vulnerable, free-floating. Then the power of the thing-turned-symbol-turned-sacrament is so great that it reintegrates our perceptions and enables us to receive thousands of stimuli that bombard our consciousness daily with a new perceptual structure. The thing-turned-sacrament has forced us to the limits of our existence, compelled us to ask some basic question about the meaning of that existence, and in the very asking we perceive, however dimly, in the thing-turned-sacrament some hint of an answer or an explanation.

Life is uncertain, fluid, drifting, random. The Church to which one was once committed is like a ship with no one at the rudder. The certainties and the stabilities of the past have been swept away. One has nothing to cling to, nothing to lean up against. Vertigo is constant. Then one sees a great massive rock against which the waves of the lake or the ocean are crashing. The rock is strong and stable; one's own existence is fragile and weak. The rock was there before one came, it will be there long after one goes. What incredible strength compared to one's own weakness. How can it be that the rock is so strong? How can the rock be so invulnerable and we so vulnerable? How can the rock be so resistant and we so prone to shatter? In that moment of question and illumination one perceives that there is strength in the cosmos which underpins the rock and underpins us too. In that strength we find our strength, we share in the same shatterproof Reality that manifests Itself so strikingly in the rock. Confusions, uncertainties, unexpected changes will no more move this ultimate strength of the universe than the waves will move the rock. We participate in some fashion in this ultimate strength, so we too are strong. Vicissitude will no more shatter us than the waves shatter the rock. We go back to the troubles of daily life with no problems solved, perhaps, but with a very different way of looking at things.

And if the rock symbol is already part of our religious life, then we go back with a new or renewed appreciation of what the rock of Peter really means, with more confidence not only in ourselves but in the Church which is built upon that rock of Peter.

This is what the psychologists and the philosophers call a "limit-experience," an experience of having reached the horizon of our existence and seeing beyond it, however transiently and intuitively. It is in the limit-experience that a thing becomes a symbol, an object becomes a sacrament, a little hunk of the everyday world becomes a revelation. The ecstasies of the great mystics are, I suspect, nothing more than superduper limit-experiences, as are the insights of poets. Even those of us who are not metaphysicians, poets, or ecstatics still have limit-experiences. Even such an incorrigible writer of prose as myself has had them or I could never describe one. My prosaic, pragmatic, and empirical spirit may be such that my experiences are rather unspectacular, but I have them, and so does everyone else. I am particularly likely to have them when I encounter one of those elemental realities that seem to become religious symbols readily in all of the world's religions, those realities which take on deep and complex meanings because they communicate almost conaturally with the depths of our psyche (what the Jungians call ''archetypes''). The primary, the elemental, the basic quickly become sacramental precisely because they are so important and so fundamental. They are, one might say, protosacramental, or presacramental, because their role in the structure of human existence is so primordial that it is virtually inevitable that they will become revelations. Water becomes the Christian Sacrament of Baptism because it had a revelatory power recognized by humans long before Christianity.

So what Patrick is listing in this stanza of ''The Deer's Cry'' is a catalogue of protosacraments, of Jungian archetypes. He includes sun, moon, earth, fire, lightning, wind, sea, rock. He leaves out only the tree and sexual differentiation. The omission of the latter is perhaps understandable given the cultural climate of his time; he must have just forgotten about the tree.

So the sun reveals the Center of the Universe as light which dispels darkness, and the moon reveals the Ground of Being as seductively attractive radiance. The fire reveals That Which Is as consuming heat and passion and warmth. The lightning reveals The Ultimate as dancing and whirling and twirling through the universe spitting off sparks of life. The wind shows us The One Who Is as blowing whither He wills, lighting down here, now there, speaking to our spirit with the invitation to the dance. The sea shows us The Absolute as unfathomable, profound, absorbing, overwhelming. The earth tells us of a God who will not go back on His pledged word, who will not repent the promises He has made, and the rock assures us that in the titanic war in heaven between Good and Evil, no power will ever shatter the ultimate strength of Goodness.

We do not see these things, of course, every time wind, moon, sun, lightning, or fire, earth, sea and rock impinge on our consciousness. The sacramentality of Being is not something that is always obvious; but it is there nonetheless, and not merely for the great mystics or even the ordinary mystic; it is available to anyone whose sensitivities and sensibilities have not been completely dulled by the cares of life and the distractions of the mass media. The Real is lurking out there behind every bush, around every corner, beneath every rock, speaking to us, inviting us, attracting us, pleading with us, trying to seduce us to the dance, or merely encouraging us to come out and play. It's there, all right. The question is not whether it's there but whether we're there. It is foolish to go down the deer path of life surrounded by a world of sacraments, a world of things crying, pleading, demanding that we permit them to be symbols, and not pay any attention.

FIFTH
MEDITATION

I arise today
    through God's strength to pilot me:
God's might to uphold me,
God's wisdom to guide me,
God's eye to look before me,
God's ear to hear me,
God's word to speak for me,
God's hand to guard me,
God's way to lie before me,
God's shield to protect me,
God's host to save me
From snares of devils,
From temptations of vices,
From every one who shall wish me ill,
Afar and anear,
Alone and in multitude.

I speak with a friend.
    In the last stanza Patrick saw the loving graciousness of God revealed in the inanimate objects of the universe, the archetypes of our unconscious. In this stanza he turns to human intimacy as a revelation of God's loving graciousness and describes God's relationship to His faithful followers as that of an intimate friend and

a tender lover. The knowledge, the insight, the eye, ear, lips, hands of God are committed to the service and protection of the one He loves. The deer path is difficult, dangerous, tortuous; but with the divine Lover making the journey with us, the snares, temptations, and ill-will recede before us as we tread the path with hope and confidence.

Patrick was not conscious, of course, that the limit-experience of sexual differentiation was at work in composing this stanza. To apply the imagery of friend and lover to the Deity is something that is so natural, so normal for humans that we hardly think twice about it. If we only speak of God as intimate friend and not as passionate lover, the climate of human intimacy is profoundly and pervasively influenced and shaped by the fact that paradigmatic intimacy is sexual love. All close human relationships have a strong sexual component whether we are conscious of it or not. The image conveyed by this stanza of "The Deer Cry" is that of a frightened, timid, inexperienced young bride being accompanied on a dangerous journey by her strong, wise, powerful, and deeply loving new husband. Such, Patrick tells us, is the nature of our journey through life.

Can we believe that it is so?

Is sexual love a limit-experience, a sacrament, a revelation? Is it indeed the sacrament par excellence, that human experience which reveals more fully and more adequately than any other the nature of the Really Real?

The Scriptures leave little doubt. From the commitment of Yahweh to His people in the twentieth chapter of Exodus, made in language of unmistakable sexual connotation, down through Isaiah, Jeremiah, Ezekiel, into the parables of the New Testament and the writings of St. Paul, and then into the tradition of the Church, particularly the liturgy of the Sacrament of Matrimony, the theme has repeated itself time after time: the love of God for His people, the love of Jesus for the Church is like the passionate love of the husband and wife who are deeply committed to one another. It is a hard saying for puritans, Jansenists, prigs and prudes to accept. There is something so earthy, so common, so vulgar about sexual love. How could God possibly be involved in something like that? How could he possibly lower himself to use such a dirty comparison?

There are three similarities between sexual love and the divine romance. First, sex is a raw, elemental hunger, and insistent demand, a primary craving; it is prerational, nonrational, sometimes irrational. When it takes possession of a person he can resist its power only with extreme difficulty, and when this raw, primal hunger is reinforced by and reinforces intense human affection, its demands simply cannot be denied. A husband and wife who are deeply in love with one another physically, psychologically, humanly are driven into each other's arms; and conflict, misunderstanding, disagreement, anger, and hurt feelings simply melt away in the face of their raw passion for one another.

Sexual differentiation as limit-experience reveals to us that God passionately hungers for His creatures and they for Him the way husband and wife crave one another. We are made with a hunger for the Absolute, and we will never rest peacefully until we possess it. That is evident enough to anyone who understands himself at all. But sexual differentiation as sacrament reveals that the opposite is true. God passionately craves us as much as, indeed far more than, we crave Him. The Scriptures are quite blunt about it. God lusts for his people the way a man lusts for the body of his woman and a woman for the body of her man. The puritans may wish the Scriptures were more discreet, but that is their problem.

The fierce hunger of the quest for sexual union is blended in a love relationship between a man and a woman with extraordinary tenderness and gentleness. The two alternate and reinforce one another. The power of our passion enables us to be delicately tender, and the act of giving and receiving tenderness enhances the passion. An ever so gentle touch conveys the fiercest passion, and the wildest embrace becomes a tender caress. Such is the paradoxical rhythm and style of human affection. Passion makes us tender; our tenderness makes us passionate.

It is precisely this passionate tenderness of God's loving care for us that Patrick reflects in the fifth stanza of "The Deer's Cry." All of God's resources, His might, His wisdom, His power, His eyes, ears, lips and hands are at our disposal to protect us, to care for us, to shower us with His love and affection. The lonely journey down the deer path is thus a honeymoon. Our life is a wedding trip.

This is not rhetorical exaggeration. This is not misty-eyed sentiment. On the contrary, if anything, the symbol of life as wedding trip underestimates the power and the passion of the divine tenderness for those who came into existence as the initial step of God's latest love affair.

We may not choose to believe that such is the case. A very considerable proportion of the human race has not been able to believe it. Life is not a love affair, a wedding trip, a honeymoon; it is a dreadful interlude between two oblivions, as Joseph Wood Krutch has put it. There is no way someone can be argued out of such a conviction, but in the final analysis there are only two choices: life is a honeymoon (filled with troubles and conflicts like all honeymoons) or it is an interlude between two oblivions. We can try to straddle the fence between those two choices, but before life comes to an end we must finally choose.

We may believe life if purposeful and loving and reject sex-as-sacrament on the grounds that such language is too blunt, the comparison too earthy (alternately, that it is too sentimental and romantic). This is our privilege, of course. No one is obliged to use a religious symbol that is not meaningful to them. However, a good deal of both the purpose of human life and the joy of human sexuality is missed if one does not wish to see that sexual differentiation is sacramental. Too blunt, too earthy, too romantic, too sentimental? The God of the Scriptures fits that description very well indeed.

The third similarity between the divine romance and human romance is that they are both impeded by the same obstacles. Shame, disillusionment, cynicism are the enemies that blight human love and come between a man and a woman. So, too, they blight divine love and come between us and our passionately tender God. Shame is the fear of giving ourselves completely, the fear that we are not good enough to give, and that in giving ourselves to someone else we will have nothing left. Shame is the refusal to run a risk because to lose is to lose everything. Shame is the reluctance to take a chance because one may not be up to the challenge of the gamble. Shame is the conviction that one is awkward, ugly, unworthy; it gives rise to the fear that if one is revealed totally all of the ugliness and awkwardness will disgust the other. Shame is the pathological need to hold back, to cut short, to hedge, to be safe, to be careful, to be prudent, to stay well within limits. Shame, above all, warns us against the dangers of playfulness and experimentation, of festivity and fantasy, because if we once get caught up in play we may do things that reveal aspects of the self that we wanted to hide—aspects which may be either the best or the worst in us, but which we cannot face.

And so we cautiously, tentatively experiment with one another, and then pull back at the slightest sign of danger. We cool it and operate within carefully prescribed limits with those to whom we are married, with our friends, our colleagues, and especially with God. Our shame permits us to give a little bit, indeed to give as much as is absolutely necessary to hold the relationship together; but we give not one bit more, because if we do we may be found out for the worthless, ugly creatures we are, and thus we may be laughed at, ridiculed, jumped on, destroyed.

In the passionately intense early phase of sexual love, shame is overcome momentarily. Much has to be revealed that has never been revealed before, but we quickly adjust and routinize our self-revelations so that there is no excitement, no adventure, no romance left in it. We do what we have to do quickly, efficiently, competently, and that is that. So, too, with God. Occasionally He may absolutely overwhelm us with his attractiveness, and lead us to do wild, mad things in response to His wonders; but then we pull back and settle for the commonplace, the ordinary, the routine.

At that point cynicism takes over, telling us that mediocrity is not only the way things are but the way things should be. Romance is a sentimental delusion; life is a serious, earnest business; there are too many important things to be done, too many major responsibilities to be discharged, too many critical obligations to be fulfilled.

We have no time to engage in the childish fantasies and festivities of the young. Romance, dreams, playfulness were all fine when we were adolescent, but they have no place in the life of a mature, responsible adult. Our sexual life is placed in a safe, comfortable routine. We get practiced at reading each other's cues and signals; we know what to do and what not to do, how much to give and how much to expect. The level at which we adjust may be substantially below what we had hoped for, but it is good, or at least good enough. Our needs are met. The demonic dimension of our personality is satisfied; we are not likely to do anything lunatic or outrageous. It may only be good, but it is good enough. Who could realistically expect more? There's too much risk involved, and sensible, mature adults simply don't take risks. There is not much excitement, challenge or adventure in such a life pattern, but those things are not part of life past the first youthful forays anyhow.

And so, too, with God. In principle, we are perfectly prepared to admit that He wants us totally, completely; that He wants that which is best in us, that which is most creative, most playful, most outgoing, most unique, most festive, most fantastic. In principle, indeed, that is what He wants. But we know, or at least we expect, that He will be satisfied with quite a bit less. On the basis of the record, in any case, it would seem that most people give Him less. One does not want to give too much of oneself to God, for if one does, God will possess everything and there will be nothing left for oneself or anyone else. If one really permits oneself to be completely caught up in the attractiveness of God, to be completely carried away by his seductive demands, then life will be a disaster. We will do crazy, absurd things like not worrying, like being joyous most of the time, like celebrating, dancing, frolicking, and clapping our hands too often. Just as we cool it and become sensible, sane, sober people in our relationships with one another, so we cool it in the divine romance. We say to God, just as we say to our human lovers, "Look, there are serious, important responsibilities and obligations I have in our common life. I simply don't have time to be festive or fantastic about you. I don't really believe you expect me to be that way anyhow. I'm fulfilling all my obligations, I'm discharging all my responsibilities. Isn't that what life is all about? Isn't that enough? You really can't expect anything else, can you?"

We are prepared to believe that in both divine and human life renewal is possible. One can always begin again; one can always start afresh; one can always fall in love a second time and go on another honeymoon. Such things are theoretically possible, of course. But practically (and when you hear the word "practically" you know that the cynic within us is beginning to take control), such things don't happen. What is done is done; life is what it is, and there's no point in trying to pretend otherwise.

At the root of both shame and cynicism is fear that if we let go we will fall into the abyss of nothingness; fear that if we take the inhibitions, the defenses, the prudishness, the anxiety, the phoniness out of our love, that love will become so powerful, so demanding that we will cease to exist; fear that if we permit the other to possess us completely, totally, in every inch of our body and every cranny of our personality we will simply stop being; fear that a complete, total, unreserved, uninhibited gift of everything that is us might be rejected, might be laughed at, might be ridiculed; fear that when we become completely and totally vulnerable, we may be shattered and broken. The payoff in human love is in direct proportion to the amount of vulnerability both lovers permit themselves to reveal. He who is completely vulnerable is completely at the mercy of the other. It is only is such a position of total defenselessness that we can begin to enjoy the full promise of intimacy. The stark terror of complete vulnerability is the inescapable price we must pay for the joy of intimacy.

So, too, with God. Until we are able to put our trust completely and totally in Him and experience that terrifying loneliness of depending on Him completely and not at all on ourselves, until then our romance with Him has not begun. One of the fundamental themes of the New Testament is the absolute necessity of putting total dependence on God. Otherwise we build our house on shifting sands, we lay up our treasure where the moth consumes and the rust destroys, and we can no more enter heaven than a camel can pass through the eye of a needle.

But still we try to pretend that it is different; we try to pretend that we do not exist in the palm of God's hand; we try to pretend that we are masters of our own destiny, that we can take care of ourselves, that we can protect and preserve our own life. It is foolish, it is absurd; but still, much of human effort is spent trying to escape from the radical vulnerability of contingent beings. In sexual love we can deny our vulnerability to one another. We can pretend that it is possible for two human beings of the opposite sex to sleep in the same bed, live in the same house, share the common life, periodically join their bodies in sexual union and still not be vulnerable to each other. After a time, if we work hard enough at our pretense, it becomes true. We no longer have the capacity to injure each other; hence we no longer have the capacity to give one another great pleasure and joy. The vulnerability inherent in sexual love has been eliminated. But with God the pretense of invulnerability is not there. We are contingent beings; God can destroy us. He brought us into existence out of nothing, He can thrust us back into nothing. The beginning of realism is the acknowledgment of that radical dependence; the next step is to understand that when one surrenders to the Hound of Heaven, one does not become more dependent but, for the first time, independent in the knowledge that one will be sustained forever in existence. To acknowledge our total vulnerability is the beginning of life in both sexual union and in our relationship with God. Either we conquer our fear of vulnerability and run the risk of dependence on God, or our fear overwhelms us, and we will never know what we are missing.

Patrick knew the assassins were lying in wait; he knew he had to make the journey; he knew God would protect him. This did not guarantee that he would not be killed; it merely guaranteed that God's love would persist no matter what happened. For the God who Patrick describes in this stanza of "The Deer Cry" is a God who Patrick knows has become so deeply involved in the love affair with His creatures that He is more "hung up" on them than they will ever be on Him. Patrick was and each of us can be as confident of God's love for us as can a woman who knows that she understands every secret need and desire of her man and can satisfy him far more effectively than anyone else. Why should she worry?

Why should we worry?

SIXTH
MEDITATION

I summon to-day all these powers between me and
those evils,
Against every cruel merciless power that may oppose
my body and soul,
Against incantations of false prophets,
Against black laws of pagandom,
Against false laws of heretics,
Against craft of idolatry,
Against spells of women and smiths and wizards,
Against every knowledge that corrupts man's body
and soul.

It is time to go home.
   The dark has settled on Woodlawn Avenue. The research center is empty, the university campus is quiet and deceptively peaceful. The guard at the door insists on escorting me to the parking lot. His caution is justified, my fear is valid. Whatever social explanations there may be for the crime rate they do not make anyone less dead if a knife is stuck into a heart for the contents of a wallet to feed a drug habit. I get into the car and drive off into the night. Chicago may be no more dangerous that the London of the seventeenth century, for example, and the Chicago Police Department is probably substantially more competent that the "watch and ward" of that era. Just the same, wise people have private security forces to make sure they get to their cars safely.

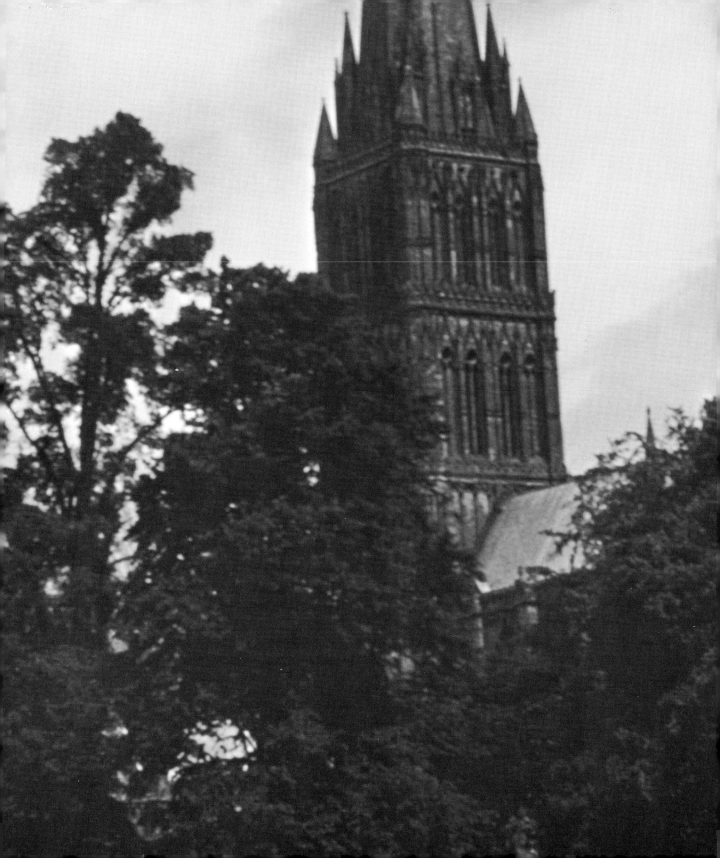

The world is filled with dangers. There is too much ozone in our cities and not enough in our stratosphere. Carbon dioxide is cooling the earth off, smog particles are making it warm up (or is it the other way around?). Virtually everything that is good (except tea) is not good for you. The air you breathe, the water you drink, the food you eat may well be filled with poisons. I guess we should be grateful that smallpox and cholera are nonexistent in this country, and bubonic plague has not got out of hand for several centuries; but then the automobile is considered unsafe at any speed, the people you encounter in the street may be potential muggers, the other nations in the world hate and envy us, there are shortages of food, energy, chromium, aluminum, iron. The IRA, the PLO, and heaven knows what other crazy revolutionary crowd may throw a bomb at you or hijack your airplane. Life is not safe. Disease, pollution, infection may get you; if they don't, criminals, terrorists or liberal ideologues surely will.

Maybe you should have stayed home after all.

At least the blacksmiths are not rebellious these days, and the wizards and women (one hopes Patrick meant witches, not all women—although he may not have been able to make the distinction) are not casting spells currently. Heretics have been abolished, and those few who are still around are now "separated brothers." Idolatry has gone out of fashion, and the only "black laws" with which pagans are harassing us at present are the export quotas of the OPEC. There are no prophets these days, either true or false. So maybe things are not quite as bad as they were in Patrick's day after all. We have at least got beyond the stage of incantations, black laws, false laws, spells and that sort of thing.

Or have we? Remember the Cambodian "incursion," "protective retaliation," "national interest," "executive privilege?" No incantations anymore? Have you ever read a manual of how to merchandise a political candidate? Or an article detailing how an advertising campaign for a new toothpaste is mounted? Ever heard somebody on a Sunday afternoon talk show who knew all the answers? Ever listen to a hard-sell pitchman in an automobile showroom? Wizards and prophets abound, and in case you haven't noticed, women's bodies are still being used to cast spells to entice you to buy automobiles, liquor, and cigarettes (which seem to be dreadfully unromantic and unimportant to me).

So it is still a dangerous world. There are people here who will try to slay us; there are thieves to take our money and goods, there are chemical, physiological, and biological dangers all around; there are pitchmen and spellbinders, demogogues and manipulators, liars, fakers, phonies, charlatans, and lunatics; there are enemies who will try to destroy our reputations; there are false friends who will betray us when we need their help; there are allies who you wouldn't want to be caught with in a dark room with the lights out.

There are well-meaning enthusiasts who are eager to provide solutions that are too simple, too pat, too easy. There are self-righteous crusaders who will destroy fragile coalitions that have been carefully put together over a long period of time. There are people who drive under the influence of liquor; there are heroin pushers and people who seem to think marijuana-smoking is virtuous.

So maybe we got rid of false prophets and heretics and idolators and smiths and wizards (the women are a little harder to get rid of), but it is not all clear that this represents much in the way of

progress. Whether the world is any less dangerous or dreadful than when Patrick and his band of monks trod the deer path, singing their hymns and confidently trusting in the Lord, but not altogether sure what they would encounter at the next twist in the road, is not at all clear. Life is still a hazardous affair, and when we stop to think of all the dangers and threats which lurk in wait for us, we most assuredly willl never get up of a morning.

There are enough things that could go wrong on any given day that if we seriously devoted time and energy to worrying about them we wouldn't be able to do anything else. Only the blind fool pretends that life is not a constant gamble. We take our chances and make sure the life insurance policy is paid up. As the Lord Jesus pointed out, worrying doesn't do any good. We cannot add a millimeter (a modern translation of "jot," I suppose) to our height by worrying about it. None of the dangers that face us—muggers, pitchmen, psychopaths in high places, the sulfur dioxide in the air —will ever go away because we worry about them. Some of them might go away because we reform our political life or improve our police protection or pass stern pollution laws, but worry doesn't accomplish any of those things—action does.

Many of the would-be prophets of our age are convinced that you have to terrify the American people to get a response. They freely admit off the record that their prophecies of doom are exaggerated, but they justify painting everything apocalyptic purple on the grounds that only such terror tactics will awaken the public to the very real dangers that actually exist. We survey researchers try to respond that the public is very well aware of the dangers that actually face us and is quite prepared to take appropriate action. If the prophets of doom accomplish anything, it is to so overwhelm many people with worry that they are paralyzed into inaction.

Some environmentalists have cried wolf so often that they have destroyed the credibility of their whole movement. They begin by trying to terrify their fellow citizens and end up by boring them.

In fact, however, it is not those who are terrified but those who are confident who are able to contend with danger. When the chips are down, when the dangers are serious, when the enemy is at the gates, you need neither the prophet of doom nor the one who is reduced to a trembling mass of jelly; you need someone with a cool head, a steady hand, a stout heart, and a strong stomach. On a dangerous journey you seek as a traveling companion neither the faint-hearted coward nor the papier mâché hero who claims not to know fear; you want someone who is very well aware of the dangers, who is quite capable of being afraid, but who can react strongly and vigorously in the face of danger despite his fears.

Only the fool denies the world is full of lurking terrors; only the coward refuses a journey; only the papier mâché hero denies his fears; only the brave man keeps his head and intelligntly and creatively responds to a real danger and the terror it generates. When Patrick and his deer pack began their journey they did not need a prophet of doom to tell them how risky it was; they didn't need a coward who would collapse at the side of the road, nor any Pollyannas to insist that there were no dangers. They needed brave men who were willing to take the chances demanded of those who live as human adults. Patrick and his band did not pretend that there were no false prophets or pagans or wizards, or smiths (what in the world do they have against smiths?), or heretics, or idolators. They were out there, all right, waiting at the crossroads with stones; but if there were all kinds of real threats to body and soul, threats of which one ought to be afraid, that was no reason to cancel the journey. They summoned up their faith and courage, invoked the saints, the patriarchs, the prophets, angels, and archangels; they took courage from the light of the sun and the radiance of the moon; they knew that God, their loving friend, was on their side throughout the journey; and so they went forth protected by their faith and also, no doubt, by a good, strong staff in hand which could be converted into a club or a shillelagh.

The Christian believes that there is nothing ultimately to fear. There may well be all kinds of forces and people in the world of which one ought to be afraid, but in the long run, in the final analysis, when all is said and done (or whatever other description you want to make of the final chapter of the human comedy), the forces and powers of darkness will recede before the banners of the Army of Light. The Christian is absolutely convinced in his heart of hearts that though he may lose some of the rounds he will not lose the match. So "Fág an bealach! Out of my way. I'm comin' down the road!"

SEVENTH
MEDITATION

Christ to shield me to-day
Against poison, against burning.
Against drowning, against wounding,
So that there may come to me abundance of reward.
Christ with me, Christ before me, Christ behind me,
Christ in me, Christ beneath me, Christ above me,
Christ on my right, Christ on my left,
Christ when I lie down, Christ when I sit down,
*   Christ when I arise*
Christ in the heart of every man who thinks of me,
Christ in the mouth of every one who speaks of me,
Christ in every eye that sees me,
Christ in every ear that hears me.

I sit down to supper.
It is the end of the day and time to eat, time to break bread. I sit down with my friends, my colleagues, with those who share community and communion with me. In the common meal we come together to know one another, and through the breaking of bread together we come to know the Lord Jesus. He has said that wherever two or three are gathered together in his name, there he is in their midst. So he is in the midst of us. Sometimes we are conscious of his presence, at other times we just barely notice he is around, and still other times we do not see him at all. If pushed, we may

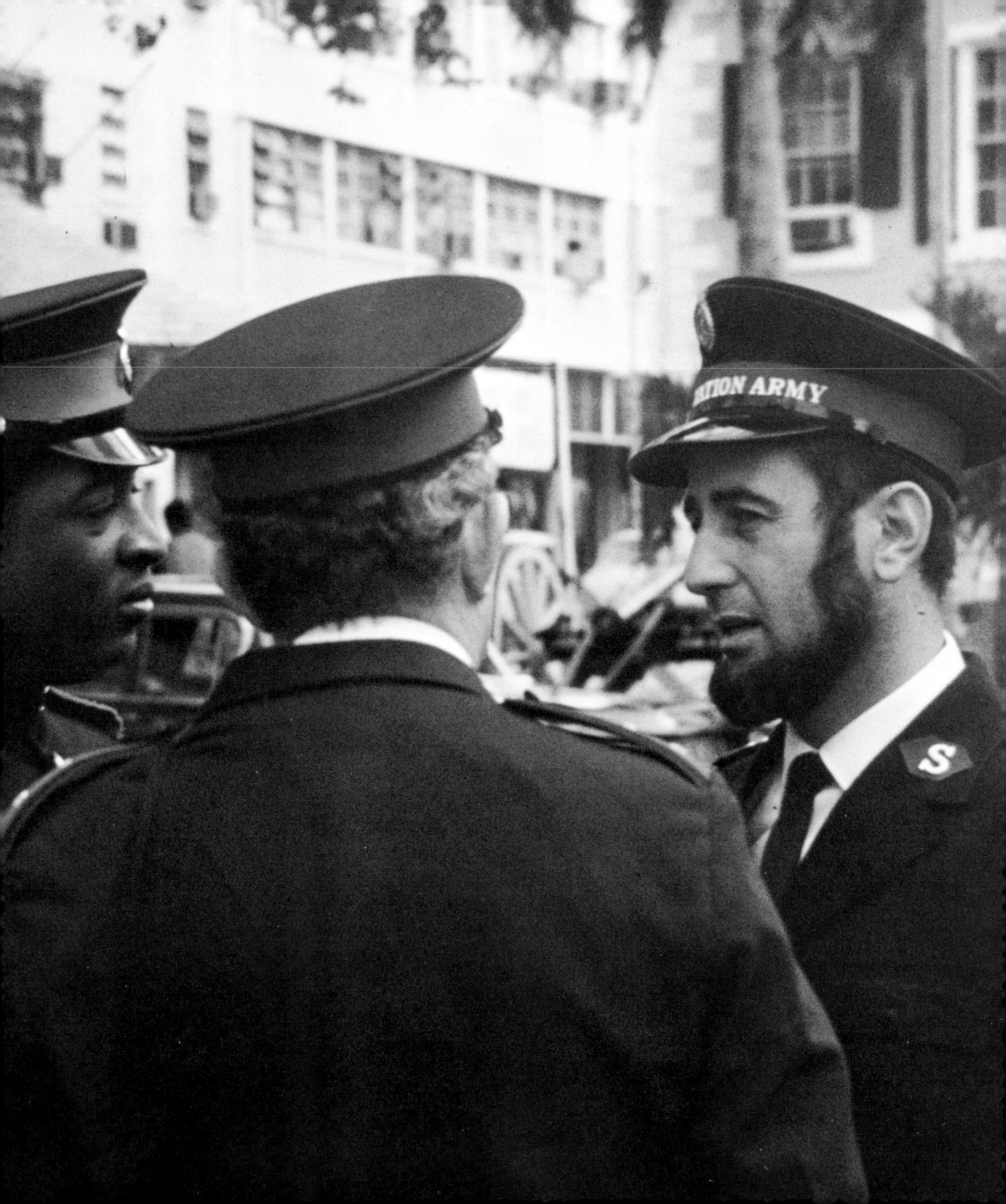
TION ARMY
S

acknowledge that Jesus is present in our Eucharist, in our common meal, and in our communal life, in our friends, families, and in the least of the brothers who calls upon us in need.

Indeed he is present as a shield against poison, against burning, drowning, and wounding, and in the heart of every man who thinks of us, in the mouth of every man who speaks of us, in every eye which sees us, and every ear that hears us. Oh, yes, that is indeed the case. We wouldn't dream of denying it for a moment. Somehow or other, though, it does not seem to be a presence that dominates our life.

Which, in a nutshell, is the difference between us and the saint. For the saint is simply a person who is far more conscious than we that Christ is present before, behind, beneath, above, on the right and on the left, when we sit down and when we arise. The saint sees Christ everywhere. The ordinary Christian admits the principle that he is everywhere, but somehow he fails to see him.

We band together in communities, I think, precisely so that we may be more conscious of the presence of Jesus. We need the support of one another in order that we may respond to the revelation of God that took place in Jesus. The Church is nothing more than a band of brothers who know they do not have the strength and resources to respond to the message of Jesus alone, and who therefore come together with one another in order that by pooling their resources, insights, strengths, they may make up for one another's weakness and respond as members of a community with the enthusiasm and commitment and in the fullness that would be hard to attain as individuals.

The most important component of this response is to be aware of the presence of Jesus. If we know that Jesus is in the midst of us, know it with the clarity that a mountain peak assumes when it is etched on a brilliant blue sky, then we can live the Christian life. If Jesus is not present in that way, undimmed by clouds of distraction, the Christian life becomes an impossibility. Hence the community we are exists principally and primarily as an institution which reminds its members that Jesus is in our midst.

In this most powerful and most frequently quoted stanza of "The Deer's Cry" we read the passionate exclamation of someone who was acutely and intensely aware of the presence of Jesus. It is the cry of a saint in the strict sense of the word, for only the saint is so consciously overwhelmed by the presence of Jesus. Such a person may not need a community to remind him of the presence of Jesus, but we who are members of a community desperately need someone like Patrick to remind us of why we exist and of what (or whom) we so often forget.

But in fact even the saint needs a community. Even saints grow weary, tired, distracted, frightened. Their awareness of the presence of Jesus may be stronger than that of us ordinary people; but they still find their efforts flagging, their bones and muscles weary, their hearts heavy and discouraged. We Christians have communities of mutual support (we call them "the Church") simply because we cannot get along without them. To band together in such communities is an inevitable part of being human; if Jesus had not intended to form a church, one would have happened anyhow simply because Jesus preached the gospel to human beings.

Unfortunately the community-called-"church" doesn't always work.

There are few greater tragedies in the human condition than the means becoming end. We band together in communities to accomplish a common goal, almost inevitably (one sociologist called it the "iron law of oligarchy") the maintenance of the community and the resolution of its internal problems and strains becomes a goal that replaces the goal for which the community purportedly exists. It does not matter whether the community is a church or a bridge club, urban government, or political movement. Eventually we spend so much time fighting those who are supposed to be our brothers in the community that we have little or no time left to achieve its goals. We cannot live without communities, but it usually turns out that we can't live with them either. A human can do very little by himself, but when he bands together with others, so much of his concern is devoted to the problems of the common life that there is not much opportunity left to pursue what was once alleged to be the common goals.

The Church is the most spectacular example of the community becoming an end in itself. The church of canon law, huge and sprawling institutional structure, rigid, authoritarian control mechanisms which medieval Christians would never have tolerated, institutionalized power structures and power elites, cliques and parties, factions and fads, rampant cronyism, corporate incapacity to respond to religious challenges is an ugly mess. What a sorry state for a group of humans who began as a band of brothers trying to respond to the message of Jesus.

To put the matter more concretely, the purpose of a liturgy is to hear the message of Jesus and respond to it in a collective celebration. At one stage of the game, when one was dealing with recent converts from barbarism, the Church had to insist on the Sunday mass obligation. Thereafter, people went to church on

Sunday because they had to and not because it was a normal, natural, and Christian thing to do. They had to fulfill the law instead of going to listen and to celebrate. Those who presided over the liturgy came to think of it as an exercise in legal fulfillment. They were there in the sanctuary so that the faithful might discharge their obligation, and it did not matter how the Word was preached, or how the thanksgiving was celebrated. Oh, it started out as a community meal of friends and fellow faithful, but it turned into an empty ritual. The important thing became to get the people in and out of mass efficiently and smoothly so that their obligation might be fulfilled. Preaching and celebration became trivial and optional components of the service. When I was a young priest the sermon had to be cut short and the Eucharist run through at breakneck speed so that the "parking problem"—the ultimate arbiter of liturgical excellence—would not create chaos. The pastor cared very little about how well we preached (so long as we didn't preach "dangerous thoughts"), and he could not have understood if someone had told him that the mass was to be a joyous celebration. The mass was something you had to go to under pain of mortal sin, and it was the priest's function to make the fulfillment of that obligation as quick and as painless as possible.

Get 'em in, get 'em out, hit the box, hit the rail, get the collection counted, the money in the bank. That was the name of the game.

Some of this has changed, but not all that much. I fear that very few liturgical services in the Catholic Church are joyous celebrations. Priests and people alike feel ill at ease with public joyous celebrations, and one need listen to the laity for only five minutes to know that although the clergy no longer have a captive audience on Sunday morning, the quality of preaching indicates that they still think they do. The institution of the clergy was developed precisely to preach and to preside over the communal celebration. Most of the clergy preach poorly and preside ineptly. They would respond in their own defense that they simply do not have time to prepare sermons or to develop a joyous liturgical style because there are so many other more pressing and more important obligations of the ministry—like keeping the books, raising the funds, administering the organizations.

In sociology we would say that the charisma has been routinized.

The means have become ends, and we have a hard time remembering what the end was. In fact, after a while, the people will think up a new end perhaps. Why do we have a church? So people can save their souls. How do we help them save their souls? By making Sunday mass readily available to them so they won't lose their souls by failing to fulfill an obligation which is binding under pain of mortal sin. It's a nice neat closed network, and it works fine until somebody comes along and mentions that the gospel is not about salvation of souls at all but about a response in love to the Good News lovingly revealed. It is most unlikely that the God revealed in the New Testament would send someone off to hell for not making it to mass on Sunday. Indeed, Jesus had a rather dramatically different set of categories to describe how his heavenly Father would decide which of the ultimate places would receive whom. "I was hungry and you gave me to eat, I was thirsty and you gave me to drink . . ."

Religious communities begin with a burst of creative insight and zeal which radiates out from the extraordinary personage of their founder. Generally even within the founder's lifetime, the internal politics of the religious community become so important that the purposes for which the community was established are quickly forgotten. Francis of Assisi was not the first religious genius to have a Brother Elias waiting in the wings.

And the small-group churches which emerged so briefly, flamed up so brilliantly and died so abruptly in the late 1960s, represented a desperate attempt of a generation of ecclesial Catholics to find a "new community" which would be more responsive to their religious needs and aspirations than the traditional parish. But the "underground church" (many of the more moderate groups rejected that name) could not survive more than a few years before they were torn apart by strife and factionalism, by personality conflict, envy and rivalry. The new communities quickly became surrogate families, and all the conflicts with parents and siblings that had remained unresolved and unrecognized from childhood were invested in the small-group church. The goals for which the group allegedly existed were quickly forgotten or, in some cases, denied. The underground church turned out to be one of the more short-lived movements in religious history.

You can't live with community and you can't live without it. Only in a community can we become adequately conscious of the presence of Jesus. We have to have two or three people gathered together before Jesus is in our midst, but it doesn't take long for the two or three to fight with one another, and Jesus is ignored. It is a paradox, an irony, a dilemma. Ultimately it is a disaster.

There are ways to combat institutionalization, routinization, the conversion of ends into means, the transference of childhood conflict into the common life. One can build into one's community or one's organization a system of mechanisms of checks and balances to minimize the impact of these destructive human proclivities. It isn't easy, and we are only beginning to understand how it can be done systematically. The fear of intimacy, of trust, of vulnerability is powerful indeed. All aggression is a form of self-defense: you do to someone what they would do to you if they had the chance.

Religiously we combat the institutionalization and the transference demons by recalling to mind that Jesus is present in the community. That recollection does not necessarily exorcise the demons. Those community members who have pathological investment in conflict will not be cured; the sticky morass of obsolescent structures in which we are entangled will not be cleared away; but as mature adults among us are aware of the presence of Jesus among us, they at least can begin to build anew. We can acknowledge the painful inevitability of human sinfulness and strive vigorously to do what we have come together to do: respond to Jesus who is in our midst.

But what does it mean to say that Jesus is "in our midst." He is present, of course, in the Eucharist. He is present through his Word that is preached to us in the gospel (however ineptly we may comment on it); he is present in that the tradition which has been handed down to us is one that takes its origin from him. He is present in the sense of mythological presence: mythological time is not quite the same as chronological time. The great saving paradigmatic acts of religion are present at all times not merely in their effects but in their powerful dynamism. The forces unleashed by Jesus are still very much at work in the world, and through them we are in actual contact with him. Time is only a minor barrier.

But is Jesus truly, really, physically present in the room when we sit down for our ordinary meal? There is one way in which he is not present and two ways in which he is. He is not present the way he was at the Last Supper or at the marriage feast in Cana. His visible physical body is not in the room; he does not sit at table and talk with us as he did with his apostles. Sometime, somehow, in some way in the Kingdom of the Father he will be present in such fashion again, but now he is not. We may pretend that he is, and there is no harm in that so long as it does not cause us to overlook the other two ways in which he is present.

It is no exageration to say that Christianity is Jesus. If one wants to know how Christianity differs from the rest of the Yahwistic tradition of which it is a part, the answer is simply Jesus. His person, his life, his preaching are what makes us distinctive as Christians. All the great moments in the Christian tradition have been developed precisely because some person or some group of persons encountered Jesus in a new, startling and dramatic way. They did not meet him, as Paul did on a horse in the road to Damascus, but through meditating on his person and his work, through listening to the tradition about him; and then by responding to that tradition with their own insights and faith they met him again just as truly as did his early followers, though in a different modality. Jesus is present among us the way Washington, Jefferson, Madison, and Lincoln are present among Americans. His thought, his life, his mission, his words, his intense attractiveness as a person has been treasured, reflected upon, prayed over, reenacted down through the ages; and so he comes to us whenever we gather together.

He is also present in the least of the brothers even as he promised he would be. He is, as St. Patrick says "in the heart of every man who thinks of me, . . . in the mouth of every one who speaks of me, . . . in every eye that sees me, . . . in every ear that hears me.'' Why is he present? He is present because you and I, we, are the objects of his love. A man is present wherever his beloved wife may be; the strength of his love for her and hers for him brings his influence into every place where she walks. The power and the force of his personality follows her wherever she goes. And what one does to her one does to him no matter how distant he may be. Similarly, the other members of our community are passionately beloved by Jesus. His strength, his power, his vigor, his goodness is present in them. Whatever we do to them we do to him.

Sometimes it is very difficult to see Jesus in the brothers and sisters. Sometimes their own fear, defensiveness, and neuroses are such that they obscure him almost totally. Sometimes we must deal firmly and vigorously with them, but even in such lamentable cases, we must also deal kindly because even if they don't seem very lovable, Jesus still loves them and is present in them. If it seems that he shows poor taste in those he chooses to love, we must simply remember that it was always so. He gathered a ragtag, faction-ridden, unpresentable band of braggarts about himself when he began to preach the gospel. The Church, it is much to be feared, has never been better than that first sorry band of brothers. As long as people like us are permitted in, it never will be much better.

But, of course, it is for people like us that it was designed.

''Ah,'' says the literal-minded modern, ''but then Jesus really isn't present in the community?''

There is no way that one can deal with such a response, though heaven knows the religious education we receive in the post-Tridentine Catholicism makes such a response almost certain. If one is to use the word ''real'' only when one is referring to a visible, physical presence, then no, Jesus is not ''really'' present around our common table. But this is a very narrow and limited Enlightenment use of the word ''real,'' and one which most people in most times in human times would not accept.

If the question is rephrased, ''Are we in mystical communion with Jesus through a variety of different mechanisms, so that he is truly in our midst whenever we are gathered together in his name?'' The answer in this case is surely yes. He is present in his message, in his saving actions, in his personal image, and in his beloved brothers and sisters. If that doesn't satisfy us, nothing will. If that is not enough to remind us that we have come together as a community to respond to his loving message, then nothing will remind us.

And if we are not content with such a presence of Jesus we better get out of the deer pack.

I arise to-day
Through a mighty strength, the invocation of the Trinity,
Through a belief in the threeness,
Through confession of the oneness
Of the Creator of Creation.

EIGHTH MEDITATION

*I should like to have a great pool of ale for the King
of Kings; I should like the Heavenly Host to be
drinking it for all eternity.*

*I should like to have the fruit of Faith, of pure
devotion; I should like to have the couches of
Holiness in my house.*

*I should like to have the man of Heaven in my own
dwelling; I should like the vats of Long-Suffering
to be at their disposal.*

*I should like to have vessels of Charity to dispense;
I should like to have the pitchers of Mercy for
their company.*

*I should like there to be cheerfulness for their sake;
I should like Jesus to be there too.*

*I should like to have the Three Marys of glorious
renown; I should like to have the people of
Heaven from every side.*

*I should like to be a vassal to the Lord; if I should
suffer distress he would grant me a good bless-
ing.* *

---

*"I Should Like to Have a Great Pool of Ale," 10th Century, translated by Kenneth Jackson in Greene, ed., *Anthology, op. cit.* This poem is generally attributed to Brigid, the great saint of the fifth century.

I throw a party.

It is time to have a party, and if I think hard enough I shall find some pretext. My parties, if I say so myself, are fun. They are based on the premise that the purpose of a party is to bring different kinds of people together. I suppose that it enriches them personally and helps them to grow if they encounter those who are different from themselves, but I confess I have no such grand and noble purpose. I simply think it's fun. So I take a sample of the remnant of the South Side Irish, a handful of people from the university a group of journalists and media people, and maybe a couple of clergy, and I mix the whole crowd together, sprinkle ever so gently with good wine and stand back to enjoy the fun.

You have to be careful, of course. You just can't invite just any South Side Irishman, Hyde Park intellectual, priest, or journalist. There are very members of each group who are so arrogant, so narrow, so rigid that they are not merely incapable of communicating with those who are different from them, but they feel so intensely superior to those who are different that communication is hardly worth the effort.

I look for those who are curious, know how to ask questions, how to listen, and how to describe what they are doing to others in terms the others can understand. At such parties one must have people who are capable of talking about something else besides themselves, and who are not so bound to the code language of their own part of the beach that they cannot communicate without falling back on its arcane vocabulary. For my parties I have to find people who are at least as interested in learning about others as they are in talking about their favorite subjects.

So the South Side Irish must divert their attention to something else besides politics and Notre Dame football, the journalists must forget about yesterday's paper or today's early evening newscast, the clergy must eschew conversation about the cardinal (in the shocked awareness that not many people care about him), and the intellectuals must discuss their work (if at all) in such a way that you don't have to belong to their guild to know what the hell they mean.

Such parties are risky, although I have never had one blow up yet. Some people think I cheat, because as the Irish become more strongly represented in journalism and scholarship, such celebrations of diversity could all too easily become diversity of occupation within the Irish community. Sprightly and vigorous conversation among a crowd of Irish is hardly a notable social achievement. The obsession of the Irish with conversation is historic if not epic.

So I guess I like parties. You can imagine what Brigid's line does to me, "I should like there to be cheerfulness for their sake;/ I should like Jesus to be there too."

He's not Irish, but he's welcome to my party any day.

Brigid's song brings us into a totally different world than "The Deer's Cry." Patrick's hymn is almost independent of time and place, a wild prayer of mystical longing which save for the references to smiths and women (I still can't figure out what he had against them) might be uttered by any mystic at any time in any place. Perhaps in the original Gaelic its Irishness is more evident, but surely in translation one is not able to apprehend where it should go in time or space.

But Brigid's hymn clearly says "early Middle Ages," indeed, "early middle Ireland." An Irish king (and anyone who owned a few head of cattle was one in those days) is entertaining a guest and his followers. Great quantities of ale are brought in so the guests may drink all night long (some things about the Irish never change). Dishes of fruit, pots of stew, vessels of food and drink, wheels of cheese, pitchers of wine are brought in and passed around. The women of the house sing songs and tell stories and recite poems and bring laughter and merriment to the assemblage. The vassals and the servants anxiously wait along the wall to do whatever they can to make the party a success.

"Drink up the ale, my guests. We have a long night ahead of us, with songs to sing, poems to compose, stories to be told before we're through." And the stories get better as the ale flows ever more freely, and the laughter rebounds off the walls where the nodding servants lean.

"Drink up, friends! There'll be no shortage of ale at my house tonight."

I am enough of a puritan to be offended when people get roaring drunk. I am not given to the "creetur" myself, and I have a bad habit of remembering exactly what everyone says under the influence of the vine—a habit which has destroyed a couple of friendships. At my parties the ale may flow all night as long as my guests can remember the next day what they have done. It does not always work out that way.

Well, *they* can go on all night long, but after 2:00 a.m. they can forget about me. I have work to do tomorrow.

But with these qualifications, Brigid's party sounds like one that would be fun to go to—particularly when the storytelling got going in ernest.

It may be a lunatic conceit: the heavenly Father sitting in front of a great roaring peat fire (does peat roar?), a mightly flagon of ale in the one hand, a shillelagh in the other, and a wild, tall tale on his lips. He might begin, for example, ''Well, one night, a night rather like this, my 'men' and I were having a party rather like this, and I got the brilliant idea that I would create humankind. Let me tell you, that was the beginning of the most incredible tale of all. You wouldn't believe . . .''

''Blasphemous!'' exclaims a priggish critic. ''Absurd!'' says a philosopher of language. ''Sentimental,'' observes a cynical theologian of liberation. ''God wouldn't drink,'' insists the puritan.

I agree with them all. Everything they say is right, just as right as if they had said the same thing about a passage in St. John that begins, ''There was a marriage feast in Cana in Galilee, and the mother of Jesus was invited. Jesus and his disciples were also there . . .''

So Brigid's song has good company.

It takes a special kind of poetic audacity to think of such a thing (though we should remember that the Lord God Yahweh did come down to sup with Abraham). But much more than audacity is required for the loving tenderness which murmers, ''I should like there to be cheerfulness for their sake.''

Heaven knows we need a little cheerfulness, but does the Lord in heaven, even should he don Irish linen, find some of the best Irish wolfhounds, gather some of his angels to come down an join our party? Why should they need or expect cheerfulness from us? We'll provide the ale and the wine and the stew, cheese, singers, and taletellers; but cheerfulness they will have to bring themselves. Even at a human party, a host can't guarantee cheerfulness. He would like to have it be there, of course, but there is no way he can be certain.

If the King of Kings and his crowd show up at one of our parties, it doesn't seem fair for them not to bring their own cheerfulness along. What good is a place like heaven if it doesn't have a super-abundance of good cheer stashed away somewhere.

But Brigid seems to think that even the King of Kings might need cheering up at a party. The good fifth-century host does all he can to ease the burden of travel his guest has just undergone. The fire is warm, the food good and plentiful, so, too, the drink; and the host does all he can to make his Irish royal guest feel at home. Above all, he tries to provide a light, cheerful, amusing, entertaining atmosphere for the pleasure of his guests.

This may all be fine for the high kings of Ireland both as guests and hosts, but obviously God doesn't need to be eased out of the weariness of a long, uncomfortable journey by a show of our cheerfulness. Does he?

Is Brigid merely engaging in a wild flight of poetic fantasy? Or has she touched on a truth of humankind's relationship with the Ultimate that we would do well to remember. The Infinite, the Absolute, Being itself may well require our cheerfulness for his own peace of mind. Even in the Whitehead notion of a suffering God, the notion of our telling tales and singing songs to amuse a God who has grown disheartened over his work seems a little bizarre. Yet it is surely the case that the King of Kings wants us to be cheerful. He may not need our cheerfulness, but he needs us as cheerful persons. Otherwise why make us, why love us, why intervene in our existence? Why begin his affair with us by thrusting us into being in the first place? If it be true that God needs us cheerful, then Brigid's poetry is not as wild or exaggerated or as maniacally Irish as it may seem. For the King of Kings under such circumstances comes to every party, and a flagon of ale better be reserved for him, the stories, songs, poems better be good, and the food better be delicious because otherwise the party will be a failure, and the King of Kings will not go home cheerful.

And he might say to his Jesus when he gets home, "Son, you didn't miss a thing."

Some parties are social and business obligations. They don't count. Some parties are occasions for compulsive self-display. They don't count either. Still other parties are ways of settling scores. They surely don't count.

But some parties are in fact celebrations. Weddings, birthdays, baptisms, Christmas and St. Patrick's Day parties are certainly to be counted. And we certainly count those spontaneous affairs that happen just for the hell of it because friends want to get together. The cheerfulness of those parties, I would submit, is the celebration of life, a celebration of the goodness, the joy, and the graciousness of life, and of our conviction that life is far too wonderful to be glum about. The best of our parties are celebrations of life, celebrations of being. Of course, the Author of Life, the Author of Being is at the party, and if he enjoys life and being (and he must, otherwise why did he create it?) then he must be having a rip-roaring good time there. If our parties are dull, morbid, anxious, vindictive little sessions, then I suspect the Lord of Life will go home very early, pleading an important crisis somewhere else in the Milky Way, perhaps.

So cheerfulness is not just an option, celebration not merely something we can choose if we want to. We have an "obligation" to celebrate, a "responsibility" to be cheerful. Thank heaven our "obligation" and "responsibility" to be cheerful are not imposed upon us on pain of mortal sin by canon law. We must be cheerful for God's sake. Parties are not just nice things to have; they are an essential requisite of the human condition. He who does not have parties and does not go to them is not really a full-fledged member of the human race. And he may miss the King of Kings who turns up at most of them these days.

So collect the flagons and the pitchers and the pots and the plates, find the ale and the wine, the cheese, fruit, and the meat for the stew, go out in the rain and dig up the peat, tell the bards to sharpen their verses, the musicians to tune their instruments, tell the storytellers that tonight we expect the greatest tales of all. There is going to be a great, splendid party, and you'll never guess who's going to come to have dinner with us!

NINTH
MEDITATION

My hand is weary with writing,
My sharp quill is not steady,
My slender-beaked pen juts forth
A black draught of shining dark-blue ink.

A stream of wisdom of blessed God
Springs from my fair-brown shapely hand:
On the page it squirts its draught
Of ink of the green-skinned holly.

My little dripping pen travels
Across the plain of shining books,
Without ceasing for the wealth of the great—
Whence my hand is weary with writing. *

I sit down to write.

"Why do you write so much?" It is a question I have never understood. Much less have I understood the tone of injury and affront with which it is usually asked.

Writing is not like eating, drinking, exercising, wenching, or any other activity which, performed in excess, might injure one's health or threaten that of others. The addicted writer's vice, if it is

---

*"St. Columcille the Scribe," 11th century, translated by Kuno Meyer in Greene, *Anthology, op. cit.*

a vice, is harmless; it injures no one save those publishers who happen to lose money on his books. Writing, it seems to me, is one of the most harmless of escapes.

"You write too much" is the ultimate condemnation. It is very like the old *ipso facto* excommunications of the pre-Vatican Church. The judgment is spoken, it is not subject to appeal, and forgiveness is reserved *personaliter* to the Holy Father.

Sometimes there is an implicit charge that quantity precludes quality. That's a little rough on G. K. Chesterton and Agatha Christie but perhaps valid. One would expect that documentation would be required. If quantity does exclude quality, then one should be able to find clear and evident errors or mistakes in theology or spirituality or social science. But in fact the incompatibility of quantity and quality is assumed and need not be documented: if you write a lot, you are bound to write badly, and that is that.

So I still don't know why literary productivity is offensive to so many people. I could suggest that they are under no obligation to read anything I write. The author of a book merely offers his wares for sale; he imposes obligations on no one. Hence there seems to be no good reason to be offended by his output. If he came around knocking on your door all the time, demanding to know if you had read his latest, then you could tell him that he wrote too damn much; but if he leaves you alone and doesn't harass you about his latest, why should his output offend you?

It beats me. In any case, when people ask me why I write so much, I answer simply, "I like to write."

This is all by way of saying that I don't have much sympathy for poor old Columcille sitting up there on Iona with his weary hand

and unsteady quill. Columcille wrote (and he wrote an awful lot, if the chronicles are to be believed) because he liked to write, and if he didn't like to write, he would not have done so. The incredibly exhausting work of writing is such that one can only do it if one enjoys the work despite the difficulties. Anyone who thinks the writer grinds out his latest effort with the ease of twirling a television dial has never seriously tried to write. The facility with words and the resulting high level of productivity does not mean that writing comes easy. Even when you are facile and professional, writing is more exhausting than skiing, or swimming, or hiking fifteen miles. One does it for the same reason one skis or hikes—one likes it.

It is also something that one should do if not doing it is not true to oneself. If in the random process of distribution of genes and early childhood experiences one comes up with the physiological, endocrinal, and personality system that makes one a writer, then it is a violation of one's vocation not to write. Not many of one's blue-black lines may be possessed of the "stream of wisdom of blessed God," and only occasionally may the "ink of the green-skinned holly" shape words that communicate in such a way that everyone must listen to the glories of God; but still the writer must try, and if he does not, then he is as bad as any creature who refuses to do what he is capable of doing. Just as Pangur Ban the cat must hunt mice, so his master, a ninth-century Irish monk, must write:

> I and Pangur Ban my cat,
> 'Tis a like task we are at:
> Hunting mice is his delight,
> Hunting words I sit all night.

[108]

Better far than praise of men
'Tis to sit with book and pen;
Pangur bears me no ill will,
He too plies his simple skill.

'Tis a merry thing to see
At our tasks how glad are we,
When at home we sit and find
Entertainment to our mind.

Oftentimes a mouse will stray
In the hero Pangur's way;
Oftentimes my keen thought set
Takes a meaning in its net.

'Gainst the wall he sets his eye
Full and fierce and sharp and sly;
'Gainst the wall of knowledge I
All my little wisdom try.

When a mouse darts from its den
O how glad is Pangur then!
O what gladness do I prove
When I solve the doubts I love!

So in peace our tasks we ply,
Pangur Ban, my cat, and I;
In our arts we find our bliss,
I have mine and he has his.

Practice every day has made
Pangur perfect in his trade;
I get wisdom day and night
Turning darkness into light.*

If Pangur Ban refuses to pursue mice, he ceases to be a cat. When the writer withdraws from his contest with words, he ceases to be true to his own nature. Pangur Ban has no choice but to pursue mice; he was born to achieve perfection in his trade. The writer, however, must practice always at his difficult task of turning darkness into light, for it is not an ability that comes naturally, but one which rather grows through the effort of years, working both day and night (and occasionally in airport waiting rooms).

If one is a writer in the American Catholic Church today, one will have trouble—lots of it. We are still not sufficiently free from the narrow envy of the immigrant years to be willing to accept someone who differentiates himself from others by doing something unusual or special. The writer can count on it. If he does more than just an occasional article, he will find himself on the margins of whatever community he thought he was a part of. The temptation is strong to say that it is not worth it and to chuck it all. Why work so hard for something that makes trouble for you? Is it not more sensible and reasonable to settle down to more ordinary and commonplace activities? Just as Pangur Ban can't stop chasing mice, a writer who is a writer just can't stop writing.

*"Pangur Ban" anonymous 9th century, translated by Robin Flower, in Greene, *Anthology, op. cit.*

I claim no special virtue in this matter. My writing proclivities are genetic, I think—at least mostly so. I did not grow up or go through the seminary with any plans to write, and while I still do not define myself as a writer (most of the time I still define myself as a parish priest), I am under no illusion that writing is one of my burdens and my obligations. To give it up would be as blasphemous for me as to Pangur Ban to refuse to chase mice. However, even if I tried it, I doubt I could do it for very long. Pangur might let one or two go by, but no more than that.

It is astonishing to me that American Catholicism has not produced more writers. Leaving aside the other ethnic traditions, we have a very strong Irish subculture within the American Church (half the bishops, more than a third of the clergy). The Irish are one of the most verbal—not to say word-crazy—people the world has ever known. This is not rhetoric or poetic exaggeration; it is the simple truth. The daily vocabulary of the ordinary Irish-speaker is 50 per cent higher than the average to be found in other languages, and the closer English-speaking Irishmen get to "the Gaeltacht" in the west of Ireland, the higher the number of words in their ordinary vocabulary. Why this should be so is not immediately clear and is surely beyond the purpose of this meditation. That it is so forces me to ask why the American descendants of this word-crazed people have produced so few "Irish culture" American writers.

We have, of course, great Irish-American writers—O'Neill, Fitzgerald, O'Connor, Power, Farrell, O'Hara, and more recently McHale and Cullinan. But most of them have only become free to write when they have broken away from the Church. Columcille and Pangur Ban's nameless master could write for the Church. In the

American Catholic environment, it seems that most people can write only when they have left the Church—even in this day when you don't have to struggle with ecclesiastical censors the way you did two decades ago.

I have had the distinctly unpleasant experience several times of meeting a person (usually a priest) at a conference or a lecture who is extremely friendly and attentive and interested in my work—or so it seems. As the conversation wears on, it becomes clear that he thinks of himself as a writer too, that he is firmly convinced that he has as much to say (and could say it better) than I do. What he lacks, he tells me, is the arrogance, the pushiness, the self-promotion, the ambition, the greed that are the reasons why I write and why I am successful at it. His non-writing is an act of virtue, while mine is evidence of moral corruption. But I am neither half the man nor half the writer he is, so for that I should be ashamed of myself.

That I may be neither half the man nor writer he is is a matter I will cheerfully concede for the sake of the argument. Only God knows for sure what kind of man either one of us is, and no one knows what kind of a writer he is because no one has ever seen his writing. I am not offended by the existence of writers better than myself. One reads those better than oneself not be offended but to learn.

Encounters with these angry, envious people are sad for me, and I avoid them if I can. I am sad because I take these people to be symptomatic of considerably many priests, religious, and laity in the American Church who have a lot to say and are not saying it. This is the kind of loss that we simply cannot afford. They may be consoling themselves with the thought that they do not have the breaks, or that they are not ambitious enough, or that they are too busy exercising their primary responsibilities, or that they lack the required capacities for self-promotion and self-publicization. My own guess, based on the talented non-writers I know, is that they are afraid to write. They are afraid of risking themselves on the printed page. Their splendid ideas have become identified with the core of their personalities. To articulate these ideas so that others can understand them, and to then put those ideas on the printed page risks having that selfhood stomped on by unfriendly readers. Better to feel superior to the self-promoting author who does write and publish than run the risk of writing yourself.

I have been blessedly free of identifying my selfhood with what I write. What I write is one thing and who I am is something else altogether. But you don't see me writing novels, do you? Now that's an area that could engage my selfhood. If I could write a good mystery story, I might well abandon everything else. I know in fiction one reveals a lot more of oneself than in a prose essay. I'm going to stick to essays, thank you.

Writers have no monopoly on fear. I have deliberately chosen to write about writers here because Columcille and Pangur Ban's monkish master are marvelous examples to trap the reader into thinking about the use of his own talents. Everyone has them, and everyone is afraid to use them. Everyone is afraid to use his talent for the same reason: in the full exercise of our unique talents and abilities we reveal ourselves, and most of us want no part of that. We will hide, dodge, pretend, deny, duck, escape, cop-out, do absolutely anything we have to do rather than let people get a good look at who and what we are. The student who cannot finish a dissertation, the singer who gets a sore throat every time she tries to put her rusty voice back into shape, the musician who never has time to perform, the artist who will go back to painting someday when he (or she) gets enough money to buy proper materials, etc., etc. A certain man went on a journey and he called three of his servants . . .

That which we have, that which we are is not our own. It is given to us, lent to us for our use. We can use it or we can bury it in the ground. The latter tactic is safe, careful, conservative, cautious; and in an ecclesiastical structure that is suspicious of any differentiation it may also look to be virtuous.

It is no more virtuous than Pangur Ban retiring from the mouse-hunting trade.

I once had an unpleasant encounter with an archdiocesan personnel board whose chairman (soon to be a bishop) vigorously insisted that people had to be willing to sacrifice their talents for the good of the Church. What a splendid example of counter-Reformation rigidity and stupidity! Talent is not given to us to sacrifice for anything. It would be much like the servant who buried his coins, saying that he buried them for the good of the Church. The king who gave him the coins never suggested that he bury them; on the contrary, he wanted the servant to use them to gain more coins. Any ecclesiastical structure that took over in the king's absence and imposed an obligation on the servant to bury coins would have blasphemously misunderstood the king's intention.

In cases of emergency, one may temporarily suspend the fulfillment of one's talent. One goes to the aid of the stricken instead of practicing the piano, one instructs those whom no one else can instruct, one helps when no one else will or can. The mentality that contends talent is something optional, something to be sacrificed as an act of superior virtue was once widely prevalent in the Church and is by no means gone today. It has a profound influence on the spiritual and intellectual life of American Catholicism precisely because it is such a marvelous theoretical underpinning for fear of self-disclosure and self-revelation.

As for those arrogant men and women who assume they have the right to demand of someone else that he or she not develop his or her talent—they are guilty of blasphemy and sacrilege. They not only make themselves equal to God, they make themselves superior to God. They tell God in effect that He made a mistake in endowing a person with a particular talent. I don't give a damn whether they are bishops or cardinals or mothers general or what they are; they are arrogant blasphemers, and the sooner we are rid of them the better. Such people strengthen an atmosphere in which self-revelation, always difficult, becomes more so and the hiding of the self, always easy, becomes more so.

So be it. But Pangur Ban and Columcille will testify against them on Judgment Day.

CONCLUSION

Delightful I think it to be in the bosom of an isle, on the peak of a rock, that I might often see there the calm of the sea.

That I might see its heavy waves over the glittering ocean, as they chant a melody to their Father on their eternal course.

That I might see its smooth strand of clear headlands, no gloomy thing; that I might hear the voice of the wondrous birds, a joyful course.

That I might hear the sound of the shallow waves against the rocks; that I might hear the cry by the graveyard, the noise of the sea.

That I might see its splendid flocks of birds over the full-watered ocean; that I might see its mighty whales, greatest of wonders.

That I might see its ebb- and its flood-tide in their flow; that this may be my name, a secret I tell, "He who turned his back on Ireland."

That contrition of heart should come upon me as I watch it; that I might bewail my many sins, difficult to declare.

*That I might bless the Lord who has power over all,
Heaven with its pure host of angels, earth, ebb,
flood-tide.*

*That I might pore on one of my books, good for my
soul; a while kneeling for beloved Heaven, a
while at psalms.*

*A while gathering dulse from the rock, a while fish-
ing, a while giving good to the poor, a while in my
cell.*

*A while meditating upon the Kingdom of Heaven,
holy is the redemption; a while at labour not too
heavy; it would be delightful!**

I go to Grand Beach to pray.
A melancholoy fellow, Columcille—not the brave Patrick singing on the deer path, not the sublime Brigid wishing for her great pool of ale (or bringing beer to lepers "because they had asked for it"), not even the master of Pangur Ban, playfully tilting with his cat. Columcille stands on the island of Iona, looking across the sea at his beloved Ireland and lamenting that land he would never see

---

*"St. Columcille's Island Hermitage," 12th century. Translated by Kenneth Jackson, Greene, ed., *Anthology, op. cit.*

again. There is time to bless the Lord and pray, time to read and study, time to recite the psalms, time to walk on the beach, time to fish, time to give to the poor; but alas, there is no time to go home. Unlike the modern missionaries from that soggy isle who can wing their way home in a few scant hours on the great 747's of Aër Lingus, Columcille on Iona would never go home. He was on a *peregrinatio pro Christo,* a pilgrimage for Christ; and while he loved Iona, he loved Ireland more. I think he sang his hymn of praise for Iona in part to console himself for the sacrifice he had made in leaving home.

The early Irish missionaries like Columcille, Columbanus, Killian, and the rest, were much more pilgrims than they were missionaries. The grim penetential spirit of early monastic Ireland demanded sacrifice. What greater sacrifice than to go on a pilgrimage, to leave one's beloved home behind forever? It was only an unintended side effect that the pilgrim monks also turned into missionaries, reviving Christianity in France and Germany in the early Dark Ages. The pilgrims and missionaries since Columcille and his crowd have been a wonder to all who know them. They are masters at traveling light, they can leave behind with seeming ease home, friends, and family to journey to such far places as Melbourne, Sidney, Aukland, Johannesburg, Brownsville, Orlando, San Diego. Perhaps centuries of immigrations have left their mark; perhaps the Irish have selectively bred men and women easily able to cope with mobility, who can shift from Cork to Price Canyon with nary a tear and scarcely a disturbance to their digestive tract. But it is a strange kind of mobility, for wherever they go they carry Ireland with them. Columcille took it to Iona and from Iona to

England where its impact was enormous though forgotten in the shuffle of the centuries. The missionaries who went forth in later generations to every corner of the world brought much that was good and some that was bad of their Irish Catholicism. They sang the praises of their new found homes, as Columcille did of Iona, but they also yearned for what they had left behind, and probably only dimly perceived how much of it they had carried with them.

It is not the sea, only a lake (though a damn big one), at which I look. Certainly Grand Beach is not Iona—though it probably has more Irishmen than Iona did. But we are a strange, pilgrim people— third or fourth generation in our adopted country and still able to maintain without conscious effort (and frequently without conscious realization) separate subcultural enclaves, albeit with moderately permeable boundaries. We still drink too much, we still talk too much, we are still tenaciously loyal to our friends, harsh and unforgiving to our enemies (though friends become enemies and enemies friends with remarkable frequency). We are a strange crowd, the last of an archaic people. We are high on fatalism, as the research evidence shows, but we are also high on hope; profoundly melancholy but with a gift of joy, we laugh at wakes and cry at baptisms. We cling to life with sheer desperation perhaps because our ancestors knew so little of it, yet we face death with unblinking eyes and the shrug of a shoulder. In each of us there is a mystic and a poet but also a cynic and, if the truth be told, more than a wee bit of a gombeen man. It's terrible thing to be Irish.

Until you consider the alternatives.

And so we live in a time between the times, admiring the smooth lines of the beach, the sound of the waves against the rock,

the singing of the birds, and the heavy waves on the glittering ocean. We lament our unfulfilled youths, the opportunities that have gone down the drain, the friends we have lost, the failures that have overwhelmed us, the mistakes we have made, the dreams that were blighted. Then in the midst of our gloom, we turn to our work and, like the self-exiled Columcille, we write hymns of joy.

You figure us out. I can't.

"But," says the Irishman, "it will soon be over. There were

great days and noble people, and splendid times and glorious events. It's all finished now. We're the last, and there will be none after us. They'll never do the things we did. It's all over. It's all finished. It will never happen again." As Fliam O'Brien puts it in his merciless satire "The Poormouth" (a "bad story about hard times" and an obvious satire of "Twenty Years A-Growin'"), "I do not believe they'll ever see my like again."

But how we enjoy it! How absolutely splendid to think that with us a great tradition, a great heritage dies. No one will come after us to sing our praises, to keep alive our memories, to remember our deeds, to continue the tradition which shaped us. Ah, with us it all comes to an end. There will be no more.

Do we really believe it? Of course not, and God help anyone else who suggests that the Irish are finished much less failed. We may chant our own melancholy epitaphs, but if anyone else should seriously suggest the same thing, they have a fight on their hands. We will be around when historians of the future consider Columcille of Iona and John Kennedy of Boston almost contemporaries.

On that note of contradiction, I abandon the Irish to their fate and go to bed with the image before my eyes of Columcille standing above the beach at Iona watching the waves crash against the rocks and contemplating his life with a marvelous mixture of melancholy and joy.

And to tell the truth, we're not often able to distinguish between the two.